THE SOCIOPATH

at the

BREAKFAST TABLE

....

Recognizing and Dealing with
Antisocial and Manipulative People

....

Dr. Jane McGregor and Tim McGregor

Hunter House Inc., Publishers
PO Box 2914
Alameda CA 94501-0914

Library of Congress Cataloging-in-Publication Data
McGregor, Jane (Jane Elizabeth), 1966-
The sociopath at the breakfast table : recognizing and dealing with antisocial and
manipulative people / Dr. Jane McGregor and Tim McGregor.— First US edition.
pages cm
Includes index.
ISBN 978-0-89793-696-5 (pbk.)—ISBN 978-0-89793-697-2 (ebook)
1. Antisocial personality disorders. 2. Psychopaths. 3. Families.
I. McGregor, Tim (Timothy), 1968– II. Title.
RC555.M34 2013
616.85'82—dc23   2013029725

Project Credits

Cover Design: Brian Dittmar Design   Rights Coordinator: Candace Groskreutz
Book Production: John McKercher   Publisher's Assistant: Bronwyn Emery
Copy Editor: Kelley Blewster   Customer Service Manager:
Indexer: Candace Hyatt   Christina Sverdrup
Managing Editor: Alexandra Mummery   Order Fulfillment: Washul Lakdhon
Publicity Coordinator: Martha Scarpati   Administrator: Theresa Nelson
Special Sales Manager: Judy Hardin   IT Support: Peter Eichelberger
Publisher: Kiran S. Rana

Printed and bound by Sheridan Books, Ann Arbor, Michigan
Manufactured in the United States of America

9 8 7 6 5 4 3 2 1   First Edition   14 15 16 17 18

Contents

Acknowledgments

Without the many people who have shared their experiences openly and freely, the problem of sociopathic abuse might still remain hidden, so we give thanks to all those who helped in the creation of this book. Special thanks for their personal contributions go to Nancy Ellen Iandoli and Colleen Fourie, and also to Debrieanna, Paul, and to those individuals who contributed but prefer to remain anonymous. We owe Nancy a further debt of gratitude for her comments on early drafts of the book.

Thanks also to Alison Gunson, founder of the Facebook group Children of Narcissistic Sociopathic Parents Support Group, and to its members, whose insights have greatly enriched the book. And we thank Simon Baron-Cohen, author of *Zero Degrees of Empathy,* for generously giving us permission to reproduce his EQ (Empathy Quotient) test.

Lastly, we would like to thank all the super-empaths out there, past and present, for showing us the possibilities of the human spirit.

Introduction

THIS BOOK IS DESIGNED to heighten awareness of the problem of socio-pathic abuse—and to equip you to spot and avoid sociopaths, or to remove them from your life.

Sociopaths are individuals with little or no conscience or ability to empathize with others' feelings. One sociopath (some people prefer the term "psychopath") in the course of his or her lifetime will affect many, many people in myriad harmful ways: bullying work colleagues, abusing children, instigating domestic violence, traumatizing friends and family through a sustained campaign of emotional abuse. Our purposes in writing this book are to reach out and offer supportive guidance to those who already have been targeted by a sociopath, and to forewarn and forearm others who want to reduce the likelihood of being a target of abuse themselves.

The book is also about harnessing your powers of empathy. On the one hand, empathic people prove eye-catching quarry to the sociopath; on the other, if the expression of empathy were more widely approved by society at large it could provide a powerful antidote to sociopathic abuse. We suggest in this book that empathy is the most valuable arsenal we have against socio-pathic abuse.

An empathic individual who challenges a manipulator often ends up the lone fighter, dealing with the sociopath unaided. The reason why empathic people are attractive targets for sociopaths is in part because they show emotion. The thrill-seeking sociopath finds them a source of stimulus as well as a potential threat. This creates what we call the "empathy trap": The empath is snared by the sociopath on account of his empathic nature.

1

The paradox is that the empathy trap can only be rendered ineffective if the expression of empathy becomes more widely approved. Apathy on the part of bystanders is often a problem in such situations for it perpetuates abuse. If we are to address sociopathic abuse in our communities, we need more people, more often, to express empathic outrage and concern. We need people to stand together and say, "No, it is unacceptable to abuse people this way!"

Sociopaths in Society

For simplicity's sake we use "sociopath" as a catch-all term. Because the medical profession continues to debate the exact features of this condition, the book does not explore it in detail. Our aim is to highlight not the condition itself, but rather the destructive effects of sharing your life with someone who has a sociopathic disorder.

Sociopaths are chameleon-like and lurk freely among us. They pose a serious threat to humankind, harming individuals, families, and communities the world over, affecting the health and well-being of millions daily. Yet, for reasons explored in this book, they exist largely unseen; and this lack of awareness and responsiveness means that the traumas they inflict upon their many targets go undetected.

Sociopaths exist in greater numbers than you might suppose, although it is hard to know for sure just how many there are. Since most estimates are derived from data based on specific subgroups like prison populations rather than the general population, and the condition has been subject to regular redefinition, estimates of sociopathy in society vary considerably. Martha Stout, a psychologist who treats the survivors of psychological trauma, informs us in her valuable book *The Sociopath Next Door* that 4 percent of the general population is sociopathic. This estimate is derived from a large clinical trial involving primary care patients in the United States, which found that 8 percent of men and 3.1 percent of women met the criteria for a diagnosis of antisocial personality disorder (ASPD), one of the terms used to describe those displaying sociopathic traits. The frequency of the condition was higher (13.4 percent for men and 4 percent for women) for people with a history of childhood conduct disorder (a precursor of adult sociopathy).[1]

Meanwhile, researchers Paul Babiak and Robert Hare estimate that 1 percent of the population have the condition, with another 10 percent or more falling into what they call the "grey zone." In their book *Snakes in Suits,* Babiak and Hare suggest that the prevalence is likely to be higher in some groups, including the business community, the philosophy and practices of which can encourage sociopathic traits such as callousness and grasping behavior.[2]

Australian psychologist John Clarke has been doing research similar to that conducted by Babiak and Hare. In his book *Working with Monsters* he reports that up to 0.5 percent of women and 2 percent of men could be classified as sociopathic (like Babiak and Hare he prefers the term "psychopath").[3] A British study has estimated the prevalence of sociopathy in the general population at just under 1 percent (approximately 620,000 people in the U.K.), although like other studies, this one found that prevalence is higher among certain groups, including prisoners, the homeless, and people who have been admitted to psychiatric institutions.[4]

As you can see, estimates of sociopathy in the general population vary from less than 1 person in 100 to 1 in 25. Even at the more conservative end of the spectrum, this translates into a possible 3.13 million sociopaths in the U.S. Worldwide it equates to a figure of around 70 million. So the fact that sociopathic abuse remains such an overlooked problem is surprising, if not shocking.

The cruelty of sociopaths finds no bounds, for there is no recourse, treatment, or punishment to permanently stop them.

Sociopath-Induced Distress and Trauma

Individuals who have been targeted by a sociopath often respond with self-deprecating statements like "I was stupid," "What was I thinking?" or "I should have listened to my gut instinct." But being involved with a sociopath is like being brainwashed. The sociopath's superficial charm is usually the means by which he or she conditions people. On initial contact a sociopath will often test other people's empathy, so questions geared toward discovering whether or not you are highly empathetic should ring alarm bells. Those with a highly empathetic disposition are often targeted. Those who have lower levels of empathy are often passed over, though they may be drawn in and used by sociopaths as part of their cruel entertainment, as we discuss later in the book.

Those living with a sociopath usually exist in a state of constant emotional chaos. They may feel anxious and afraid, not knowing when the sociopath will fly into a rage. The sociopath, meanwhile, carries on untouched, using aggression, violence, or emotional bullying to abuse his or her partner. Sociopaths are often aggressive, though not all of them exhibit violent or criminal behavior. Nor is aggression limited to men; sociopathic women can be aggressive and violent, too. Sociopaths make up 25 percent of the prison population, committing more than twice as many violent and aggressive acts as other criminals do. Violent sociopaths who cheat on their partners or defraud people are the ones most likely to get caught. According to Robert Hare, the author of *Without Conscience,* in the United States approximately 20 percent of male and female prisoners are sociopaths. They are responsible for more than 50 percent of all serious crimes. When they get out of prison, they often return to crime. The reoffending rate of sociopaths is about double that of other offenders, and for violent crimes it is triple.[5]

As well as sometimes inflicting physical trauma on others, there is the less visible burden of sociopath-induced emotional trauma, which if left unchecked can lead to anxiety disorders, depression, and post-traumatic stress disorder (PTSD). Chronically traumatized people often exhibit hypervigilant, anxious, and agitated behavior. They may also experience insomnia and assorted somatic (bodily) symptoms, such as tension headaches, gastrointestinal disturbances, abdominal pain, back pain, tremors, and nausea. Exposure to and interaction with a sociopath in childhood can leave lifelong scars, including a deep distrust of other people and anxiety in social situations. Yet for all these problems, no one knows the true extent or depth of mental anguish suffered by those on the receiving end of chronic sociopathic abuse, because in the majority of cases the physical and mental health problems either go undetected or the root cause is overlooked.

We believe that sociopathic abuse thus has a substantial public health dimension and as such warrants far more attention than it currently attracts. The public needs to be more alert and equipped to counter the problem and to stop sociopaths from interfering in adverse ways in other people's lives.

Furthermore, effective responses and interventions are required to reduce the range and extent of sociopathic abuse suffered by people the world over.

Chapter Summary

This book alerts you to the ruses and manipulations that sociopaths use and shows you how to invest in your empathic powers to keep them at bay. In Chapter 1, "Everyday Sociopaths," we summarize how the concept of sociopathy has been defined through the ages, and we introduce the telltale signs of sociopathy and sociopathic abuse by providing accounts drawn from real-life situations. In Chapter 2, "A Profile of the Sociopath," we scrutinize the character of the sociopath in order to help you see the problem behavior for what it is. We hope that by reading the narratives and information about sociopaths' common traits you will begin to understand the characteristics of the sociopath and of sociopathic behavior.

Chapter 3, "Sociopathic Interactions," analyzes sociopaths' relations with other people, and in particular introduces the concept of what we call the Sociopath-Empath-Apath Triad (SEAT for short). This is important to appreciate because sociopaths' interactions frequently involve not only the chosen target (often a person with a high level of empathy) but also an apathetic third party (whom we refer to as an "apath"). How these three players interact is discussed in detail, as is the unfortunate reality that sociopaths frequently enlist the help of apaths in their cruel sport.

Chapter 4, "Coping in the Aftermath of a Destructive Relationship," is about the early days following sociopathic trauma. In this chapter we include things to watch out for and ways to deal with the immediate aftermath of an association, friendship, or intimate relationship with a sociopath. In Chapter 5, "Establishing Boundaries and Regaining Control of Your Life," we focus on the process of recovery and look at measures to help you get your life back on track. In Chapter 6 we discuss complex family situations, including divorce, difficult grandparents, and sociopathic traits in children. Chapter 7 explores the potential for long-term recovery from sociopathic trauma. The book's final pages include a list of Resources such as useful organizations, websites, and books.

CHAPTER 1

Everyday Sociopaths

How do sociopaths work, and how can you spot them in everyday life? The purpose of this chapter is to heighten your awareness of the nature and variety of sociopathic behavior. Many sociopaths wreak havoc in a covert way. They may possess a superficial charm that diverts attention from the more disturbing aspects of their character. Another reason why their real natures remain hidden is because many of their behaviors are seen in ordinary people, too. Quite a lot of people cheat on their partners, have addiction problems, steal, or lie, but not everybody who does so is sociopathic.

Nevertheless, sociopaths are more numerous than is generally suspected, and you probably encounter them on a daily basis, even if you don't register the fact. They may be your neighbor, your boss, or the person next to you in the checkout line. So it is quite probable that even if you don't know a sociopath intimately, you have had fleeting contact with a few.

Defining the Problem

As we stated in the Introduction, this book is not about sociopaths or the condition per se; it is about surviving the harm they cause. We will set out to define the condition only loosely, because we aren't convinced that current terminology and labels are especially useful. The distinctions between labels like "sociopathy," "antisocial personality disorder," "borderline personality disorder (BPD)," "narcissistic personality disorder (NPD)," and "psychopathy" are blurred and confusing.[1] In fact, we hope that at some point psychiatry will move away entirely from the existing labels and redefine them all as conditions of low or zero empathy—something we discuss further in this section. Nevertheless we feel that some discussion of the changing conceptualization of sociopathy is justified, so we'll highlight some key points in the history of defining the problem.

The idea that there are people who lack humanity, who exist without empathy or concern for other humans, was first mooted in 1801 by the physician Philippe Pinel (1745–1826).[2] In his work *A Treatise on Insanity,* Pinel named the condition *manie sans délire,* which, roughly translated, means "madness without delusion." Some time later an English doctor, J. C. Pritchard (1786–1848), ascribed the term "moral insanity" to the condition. Pritchard described it as "a form of mental derangement in which the intellectual faculties [are uninjured] while the disorder is manifested principally or alone in the state of feelings, temper, or habits.... The moral principles of the mind...are depraved or perverted, the power of self-government is lost or greatly impaired, and the individual is...incapable of conducting himself with decency and propriety in the business of life."[3]

Nearly a hundred years later, in 1941, American psychiatrist Hervey Cleckley published *The Mask of Sanity,* a book that first described the diagnostic criteria for the "psychopathic personality." It was based primarily on experience with adult male psychopaths hospitalized in a closed institution. From his observations Cleckley drew up a set of diagnostic criteria, including superficial charm, a lack of anxiety or guilt, undependability or dishonesty, egocentricity, an inability to form lasting intimate relationships, a failure to learn from punishment, poverty of emotions, a lack of insight into the impact of one's behavior, and a failure to plan ahead. Interestingly, his definition of a psychopath made no reference to physical aggression or breaking the law.

From our perspective, Cleckley's best definition of psychopathy comes in a later edition of the book, in which he described a psychopath as "a biologic organism outwardly intact, showing excellent peripheral function, but centrally deficient or disabled."[4] We like both the elegance of this description and the way it pinpoints the difficulty of spotting sociopaths given their ordinary outward appearance.

Subsequent to Cleckley's book, revisions of the classification were made by the American Psychiatric Association (APA). The classification of "psychopathic personality" was changed to that of "sociopathic personality" in

1958. In 1968 it was changed again to "antisocial personality." After this, Robert Hare elaborated on Cleckley's work to create the Psychopathy Checklist (PCL) and later a revised version, the PCL-R, which became the "gold standard" assessment measure used to diagnose psychopathy. The PCL-R, which remains the standard measure today, identifies as typical of the psychopath interpersonal deficits such as grandiosity, arrogance, and deceitfulness, affective deficits (lack of guilt and empathy), and impulsive and criminal behaviors.

Hare stated that the difference between the terms "psychopathy" and "sociopathy" "reflects the user's views on the origins and determinants of the clinical syndrome or disorder." In other words, some experts are convinced that the condition is forged entirely by social forces and call the condition "sociopathy," whereas others are convinced that it is derived from a combination of psychological, biological, and genetic factors and hence prefer the term "psychopathy."[5]

Debate surrounding sociopathy and psychopathy and whether they are the same or different conditions continues unabated today. The International Classification of Diseases diagnostic criteria of the World Health Organization (ICD-10) do not include psychopathy as a personality disorder, and neither psychopathy nor sociopathy is currently referred to in diagnostic manuals, though both terms are widely used by mental health professionals and the public alike. In medical circles in recent years both terms have been replaced by the term "antisocial personality disorder," although controversy regarding the definition of the disorder continues in debates over the American Psychiatric Association's new edition of the *Diagnostic and Statistical Manual of Mental Disorders V* (DSM-5). The previous edition (DSM-4) placed emphasis on ASPD, but the criteria for ASPD lack some key elements of sociopathy and psychopathy, with some experts regarding the definition in DSM IV as describing criminality rather than sociopathy. Plenty more people can be diagnosed with ASPD than with sociopathy or psychopathy, leaving the condition closer to the parameters of "normal" human behavior. In contrast, the terms "sociopathy" and "psychopathy" help maintain the idea that the condition is distinct and extreme, hence serving to reassure the rest of us that the problem exists only in small numbers and at the margins of society.

Adding to the debate, some theorists speculate that people behave cruelly not because they are intrinsically evil (a concept many consider outmoded), but because they lack empathy. According to Simon Baron-Cohen, an expert in developmental psychopathology at the University of Cambridge, limited or zero empathy may result from physical and psychological characteristics, but empathy deficits can be turned around if people are taught to be more empathic. He points to the need to identify treatments that will teach empathy to those who lack it (as yet none are available, but trials are currently being conducted with families of children with conduct disorder, a precursor to adult sociopathy).

Putting empathy under the microscope—or rather the modern-day gadgetry of functional magnetic resonance imaging (fMRI)—Baron-Cohen explores new ideas about empathy in his book *Zero Degrees of Empathy*.[6] He suggests that the level of empathy most of us experience varies according to the conditions we face at any given moment, although all of us have a predetermined level of empathy which we generally return to (our preset position, if you like) on what he calls the "empathy spectrum." This spectrum ranges from six degrees at one end to zero degrees at the other. Highly empathic people are located at six degrees, sociopaths at zero degrees. For his research Baron-Cohen constructed an Empathy Quotient or EQ test that is intended as a measure to determine how easily you pick up on and how strongly you are affected by others' feelings. It is accessible online, and we have also included it in the Appendix of this book.

Baron-Cohen suggests that deep in the brain lies what he calls the "empathy circuit." It is thought to involve at least ten interconnected brain regions, all part of what is termed the "social brain." The first is the medial prefrontal cortex (MPFC), which is thought of as the "hub" for social-information processing and considered important for comparing your own perspective to someone else's. Baron-Cohen suggests that the functioning of this circuit determines where we each lie on the empathy spectrum. This idea relates to the earlier work of Giacomo Rizzolatti, a renowned Italian neurophysiologist. Rizzolatti demonstrated the existence of a system of nerve cells that he called "mirror neurons." His work with primates showed that these nerve cells were fired not only when an animal performed an action, but also when it saw another animal performing the same action. This suggests that empathy involves some form of mirroring of other individuals' actions and emotions.

Using fMRI, scientists have identified which regions of the brain appear to be involved in the mirror neuron system.[7]

Scientists have been quick to equate mirror neurons with empathy, but this may be pushing the idea too far. We are still some way from understanding exactly how social and biological determinants interact. Besides, mirror neurons may just be the building blocks for empathy. Other mechanisms may be involved and may be just as, if not more, significant. For instance, one region of the brain, the amygdala, is considered to be important in the empathy circuit (in fact, we have two amygdalae in our brains, one in each hemisphere). The amygdalae appear to play a key role in emotional learning and regulation processing, and are vital in cueing us to look at other people's eyes when we want clues about their thoughts and emotions.

We are encouraged by the prospect that in the future, wherever an individual sits on the empathy spectrum, he or she could be taught to be more empathic. If interventions and strategies were in place to build individual and collective empathy, then we might expect to see benefits for whole communities. If people learned to express empathy more freely, they could use it to rail against abuses of all kinds and to respond proactively to the ill-treated. Greater empathy would provide a way out of the empathy trap.

Case Histories

The accounts of sociopathic behavior that appear in this chapter are drawn from real-life situations. Although they do not constitute a complete narrative of sociopathic conduct or encounters, they are generally representative. As we've said, sociopaths come in all shapes and forms—men, women, and even children—and can be hard to spot. We hope these case histories illustrate how individuals may be systematically targeted until they feel they can barely trust their own sense of reality—a phenomenon we call "gaslighting" (see Chapter 3). Sociopathic abuse is targeted abuse. Sadly, it can wreck lives, though we also hope to show that victims, with time and healing, can become survivors.

Throughout the book, most individuals' names have been changed to protect their identities.

♦♦♦ The Sociopathic Spouse

Susan, age forty-seven, was an elementary-school teacher. A placid, kindly woman, she used her job as an escape from home, where her husband, Peter, ruled. A retired teacher who still worked occasionally as a substitute, Peter was spending increasing amounts of time at home. Once she'd cooked him breakfast and he'd approved her clothes for the day, she was free to go; her salary, paid into their joint account, was a welcome supplement to his income. (He profoundly disapproved of her maintaining her own bank account, in which she was only allowed to keep a token amount.) Peter didn't want to hear too much about her day when she returned home. He was often moody or sulky—or off playing golf—but he expected her to cook supper when he was ready for it.

Control, and being in control, is of key importance to sociopaths. Peter was never physically violent, but he would erode Susan's self-confidence with constant criticisms—of her weight, clothes, appearance, and achievements in general. "I was always being measured and assessed, and usually just not doing well enough. It was like living with a school principal who was always grading you," she said. He tried to control which friends she saw—in fact, he preferred that she not see any. Likewise, early in their married life he had tried to cut her off from her family, saying that her parents had personality disorders and her sisters were fools. He displayed another typical sociopathic trait: he was hypercritical. No one was ever good enough, and as a couple they were socially isolated. But Susan's naturally sociable nature prevailed, and she managed to maintain friends and a social circle away from home. Still, in many ways it was a lonely life, especially because Peter was also physically distant. Whatever intimacy had once existed between them had long since dwindled. If Susan pushed for change, Peter became threatening and aggressive.

Susan dearly loved her students, but her job wasn't enough to ease her growing restlessness. She did something that seemed entirely out of character: She had a brief liaison with a social worker at her school. She was not much good at cheating, so the affair ended quickly and she confessed everything to Peter. Peter said little at first, but soon he took his revenge; he told their three children about Susan's affair. Although the children were adults who lived away from home, they felt the bond of trust with their mother had been destroyed, and that she had behaved abominably. Peter also told them that Susan had neglected them as children, that she was an alcoholic, and that she had behaved erratically and cruelly toward him. Being highly articulate and forceful, Peter talked the children down if they ventured to doubt the stories, and said that Susan had done a good job of deceiving them.

Susan was devastated. For twenty-five years her life had revolved around her family's wants and needs and, in particular, around Peter. She believed her life was over, and that none of her children would ever trust her again. Peter announced that he was leaving, and that he would fight Susan for the house and their money. But Susan got a good lawyer and managed to secure her rightful share of their possessions. While sorting through papers, she came across some that revealed that Peter himself had had several affairs. Another common hallmark of sociopaths is secrecy and a double life. It turned out that when Peter was "playing golf," he was often socializing with people whom Susan had never met, including both a mistress of many years' standing and more-casual liaisons.

Susan's life took a lot of rebuilding, but with the support of friends and the help of a counselor she is coming to terms with the aftermath of her marriage. She began seeing a man named Gerry, who proposed marriage. Because she felt she needed some time on her own, Susan refused, but said she'd reconsider in two years' time. Meanwhile, they're developing a friendship based on mutual respect. She is also rebuilding her relationship with her children—and trying to get them used to the fact that she is no longer the doormat she might have been when they were growing up.

♦ ♦ ♦ The Sociopathic Parent

The following is Rebecca's story, told in her own words:

> Motherhood did not come naturally to my mother. It took me several years to realize that she genuinely didn't feel any real affection for me as a baby—she felt trapped, felt tied down, and hated most aspects of child-care. This might happen to any new mother, but in our case there was much more to it. She never got used to parenthood, which she referred to as the "life sentence." I think she always regarded me as a nuisance; it took me a long time to realize that she disliked me just for being what I was. She was cold and distant. She had fits of vindictive rage in which

she would beat me and lock me in a cupboard under the stairs; once, she hacked off chunks of my hair. She repeatedly told me I was worthless, and with time I came to believe it. To divert attention from the abuse, she ensured that I was always well dressed—though few people got to see us out and about together. As another distracting device, she developed an extreme case of agoraphobia and other psychosomatic (I now think) disorders, took antidepressants by the fistful, and spent a lot of time in bed. We were quite isolated from the world, and I assumed this was how it had to be.

My father adored me, and I adored him. He could not help, however. He was a mild, kind man, not very ambitious, and my mother had only agreed to marry him if he provided her with the very best. Because he loved her dearly, he worked like a slave. My mother grew to resent the attention my father gave me, and did all she could to keep us apart, but when he came home at night and showered me with hugs and kisses, I was happy. He was totally oblivious to Mom's resentment and to all the manifestations of the abuse, including the injuries and bruises. I tried hard not to rock the boat and said nothing. The bruises were largely hidden behind my expensive clothes.

The abuse continued all through my childhood and by the time I was in my late teens I was emotionally spent. What saved me from despair was my passion for learning. I finished school with excellent grades and secured a place at a university many miles from the family home, where I flourished.

At university I met and married Mike. Mike also had had a troubled upbringing and came from a broken home. I believed that our shared experiences and understanding of life meant we were the perfect match. After college we both found good jobs, and everything seemed to be working out. But I found marriage lonelier than I expected. Our perfect understanding didn't last—Mike took to drinking and became violent and aggressive toward me, even during my two pregnancies. Furthermore, there was a growing distance between my father and me. My mother employed all manner of tactics to block contact—she intercepted mail, arranged long weekends away when I wanted to visit, and always answered the phone. Dad and I seldom spoke, and I came to believe that he was rejecting me.

Over the next few years Mike and my problems escalated. So did our debts after Mike lost his job because of his drinking. I had no one to turn to, and had more or less lost touch with my parents. Then one day, out of the blue, my mother called and said my father was ill, and that she needed my help paying the bills. I tried to explain that we were deeply in debt ourselves, but the call ended in a horrible argument.

I never saw my father again. Six months after that phone call, he died in the hospital. My mother didn't tell me until the next day. When she did call, it was to inform me that she'd persuaded Dad to write me out of his will.

Viewed from one perspective, sociopaths, whether men or women, appear to get away with their abusive behavior, leaving scars of various sorts in their wake. Yet looked at from another angle, their behavior comes at a great cost not only to others but also to themselves. Rebecca's mother never saw her grandchildren; indeed, Rebecca was determined to protect her children from the possibility of her mother's abuse. There seemed to be a whole dimension of life to which Rebecca's mother was blind. With time and a great deal of counseling, Rebecca was able to reach this dimension and to see that life was a larger and kinder affair than she had found it as a child.

◆◆◆ The Sociopath at Work

Mary narrowly escaped becoming deeply entangled with a sociopath, although she didn't realize it at the time. As an office receptionist, she was exposed to the full force of her coworker John's "charm"; he paid her compliments about what a sterling job she did, and he made comments meant to evoke her sympathy about how hard he worked. He gave her rides home, during which he talked with a sad face about how his boss was against him and did everything he could to block John's career. Widowed at a young age, Mary had no plans to remarry and did not go out of her way to attract men, but, with John, she might have been tempted. Vistas of a new life opened before her—and once they had appeared, it was hard to ignore them. She began to dress more stylishly, lost weight, and had her hair colored and permed.

Being bright and observant, she watched John with some attention. It all seemed a little too good to be true. She noticed that he could drop the charm like a cloak when he wished, revealing a very definite, almost dogmatic manner beneath. She observed how he flirted with Kylie, the office beauty (who, wisely, didn't respond to his advances), and how often he looked at himself in the mirror. John "accidentally" dented his boss's new car while parking one morning and managed to get Kylie blamed for the event. He spread a rumor that Kylie had been brought in by central management to close the office. His tensions with his boss escalated, and John finally lodged a formal complaint of unprofessional conduct against him. Mary began to have doubts about John. Magnetic as he was, he seemed to attract just a little too much trouble—though she did find it pleasant to be confided in and told how understanding she was.

John's comeuppance eventually came from an unexpected source—the SPCA. Neighbors had notified them that he treated his young Labrador badly, keeping her locked up in the garage all day with inadequate water and food. It turned out that he only had possession of the dog to hurt his ex-wife, who adored it. All of this came to Mary's attention via a neighbor, and when she asked John about it, the mask slipped. He stuttered out some excuse about the dog's being ill, but Mary had seen through him.

For Mary, the positive effect of coming into contact with John was feeling that she could perhaps be attractive to men again after having lost her husband. On the negative side, her confidence was severely dented. She doubted her ability to make wise choices in relationships, and felt she had been a "dupe" to have been so deliberately used in one of his complicated games. Mary felt relief at being rid of this "charmer," but she also believed she should have seen through him earlier. Her hurt lasted for quite some time.

♦ ♦ ♦ The School Bully

James, fifteen, was an only child, privileged, bright, and supremely confident. Despite his undoubted advantages, however, he was often bored and listless, skipping school with faked illnesses and finding it easy to manipulate his parents. At school James took a dislike to a classmate, Sam, who was sensitive and popular. James would mock Sam for auditioning for a part in the school play, or for getting upset over failing a geography test. The situation deteriorated when it became known that Sam's parents were separating. Sam appeared to be taking it all with fortitude, to the admiration of his peers. Sam also got attention and sympathy from the school staff, especially from James's "favorite" teacher—or the teacher he found easiest to manipulate.

Using the class gossip, James started a whispering campaign implying that Sam's parents weren't splitting up, and that he had only said they were in order to seek attention. As a result, over the next few days Sam was met alternatively with silence and verbal bullying from his previously support-ive classmates, a situation that escalated into a physical fight in which Sam was knocked out. James continued his campaign, targeting several of Sam's close friends. They found themselves accused of serious misdemeanors such as stealing money and sending offensive e-mails and text messages. Then James's "favorite" teacher was put on administrative leave after being accused of physically assaulting a pupil. James had falsely made the accusations.

While it seems hard to believe that one young schoolboy could cause such havoc, James's story demonstrates how deliberately sociopaths can and do target others. Taking advantage of people's general credibility and good-will, and of the school's structure and culture, James exploited the situation with almost uncanny insight and destructive flair. With a more perceptive principal, James might have been found out, but like so many sociopaths he knew just whom to manipulate and how far he could go. He has since left the school, his parents claiming he "wasn't understood" there, and continues his activities in a new environment.

◆ ◆ ◆ ◆ ◆ ◆

In the next chapter we'll explore the characteristic behaviors of everyday sociopaths like the ones described here.

CHAPTER 2

A Profile
of the Sociopath

To deal with sociopaths effectively you first need to open your eyes—which is why, in this chapter, we'll be putting the sociopath under the microscope. In the tale "The Emperor's New Clothes," by Hans Christian Andersen, two weavers promise the emperor a new suit of clothes that is invisible to those who are stupid and unfit for their positions. When the emperor parades before his subjects, all the adults, not wishing to be seen in a negative light, pretend they see the emperor's elegant new clothes. The only truthful person in the crowd is a child, who cries out, "But he isn't wearing any clothes!"

In this chapter we'll help you see sociopaths in the same way the boy in the tale sees the emperor—naked, and as they really are. Very young children often have this ability. When they see behavior that defies the social boundaries they've been taught, they'll say things like "That's unkind, stop it," or "I'm telling on you, you bully." But as children get older, most find it harder to take such a bold stance. From infancy we are trained to "toe the line," to conform to society's standards and rules. We are conditioned to keep quiet, which often means turning a blind eye or putting up with abuse. The boy in the tale represents those who see the problem behavior for what it is and find the courage to make a stand. "Sight" becomes insight, which turns into action. Awareness is the first step in limiting the negative effects of contact with a sociopath.

Traits of the Sociopath

Sociopaths have certain destructive characteristics in common. However, as you probably gathered from the case histories in the preceding chapter, not all sociopaths necessarily display each of the following qualities in equal measure. Some seem to "specialize" in certain patterns of harmful behavior.

◆◆◆ Superficial Charm

Have you ever come across someone with magnetic charm, yet who also affects an air of importance and has a grandiose view of himself? Sociopathic charm is not like any other. It is not in the least self-conscious. Sociopaths rarely exhibit social inhibitions, so they hardly ever get anxious or tongue-tied. Nor are they afraid of offending you. They aren't held back by the social convention that ensures most of us take turns in talking. They talk *at* you, confident that you will agree with everything they say.

Often they have a lot to say. A "conversation" with a sociopath can feel like a bombardment. To the untrained ear, sociopaths' pronouncements sound authoritative because they tend to use words and phrases intended to make them seem knowledgeable but that upon dissection may prove to be nothing more than nonsense. This peculiarity in their mode of expression can be exacerbated by their use of muddled phrases and mixed metaphors. No one really knows why this is the case, but it seems to be a common feature.

When you first meet a sociopath, you may be impressed by her good manners. She tends to be charming at first, may go out of her way to please you, and often falls back on flattery. These tactics are designed to draw you in. But beware, for she is not what she appears, which is why sociopaths are often called "social chameleons." It seems counterintuitive that someone so charming can be so dangerous, but many people are duped this way. Being charming is a sociopath's most potent trait. Targets often later remark that they were overwhelmed by the sociopath's charm offensive. He may seem larger than life, a go-getter, an adventurer. His grandiose air and smooth conversational style add to the illusion of being in the presence of someone special. He makes you feel boring and insipid by comparison.

Everything a sociopath does is calculated to have an effect on you. Just as his charm is superficial, so is everything else about him. The smile *looks* phony because it *is* phony. The sociopath has blunt emotional reactions and fakes emotions to appear sincere. Occasionally you might catch him looking closely at your mouth as you speak, as though mouthing words and rehearsing. One commonly observed habit is a frequent pursing of the lips, chewing the sides of the mouth, or twisting and contorting the mouth in peculiar ways. It is not clear why sociopaths do any of these things. Perhaps they are practicing facial expressions, or perhaps there is some physical explanation. But the only natural smile you will see exhibited by a sociopath is a sneer as he derives pleasure from seeing others suffer.

It is hard to recognize the shameless. In her book *The Sociopath Next Door*, Martha Stout claims that the sociopath makes it his business to know how a person can be manipulated; hence his use of flattery and charm.[1] It is quite common for sociopaths to create a sense of similarity and intimacy. They will tell you that you are the only person who understands them, that you are their special "soul mate." In the case histories from the previous chapter, all the central characters possessed this quality in varying degrees. John, the workplace bully, was a master of flattery. He complimented Mary in order to "play" her and to involve her in his sociopathic games. The schoolboy, James, possessed a phony charm. He used it to blindside those in authority. As a consequence, no one guessed that he was manipulating everyone behind the scenes. In other sociopaths, such as Peter, the "charm offensive" is more muted.

◆◆◆ Need for Stimulation

Another characteristic of sociopaths is their need for constant stimulation. They become bored easily, perhaps because their emotional repertoire is so limited. Their heads are not full of the kind of emotions that distract the rest of us. It is hard to imagine what life must be like without constant emotional "noise." The rest of us have it, though we are not always aware of the fact. Occasionally this emotional noise comes to the fore, maybe when we're stressed or anxious over an exam or an illness, or when experiencing bereavement— that is, when we are far more aware of the emotions stirring inside of us.

Sociopaths, on the other hand, have a very limited emotional range and are noted for their shallowness and fleeting attachments. Consequently, they don't understand other people's "neediness" and see no point in showing emotions or sharing feelings except as an act of manipulation. Instead, and to fill the void, they tend to seek stimulation from external sources. They engage in "mind games" (struggles for psychological one-upmanship) and employ behavior to either demoralize or falsely empower their target. In this way they undermine their target's confidence in their own perceptions. The sociopath may invalidate the other person's experience—both its significance and the person's actual recollection of events—making her feel guilty for her views. Such abusive mind games may include discounting (denying the other person's reality), diverting, trivializing, undermining, threatening, and anger.

The sociopath's need for stimulation is illustrated in the case history of James, who often got bored and played mind games to relieve that boredom. John, the workplace sociopath, was in constant need of stimulation, too, and hurt others simply for the fun of it. He also had a strong competitive streak, another feature of the sociopath. Not all competitive people are sociopathic, clearly. What we are talking about is aggressive behavior in which the sociopath misuses others to dominate rivals and pushes ahead regardless of whether people get hurt. Because they are indifferent to others, sociopaths fail to display a proper sense of social responsibility. They develop strategies that allow them to ignore social convention, reason, and evidence in the pursuit of some personal goal. Sociopaths may well believe they exhibit extraordinary social responsibility, and unfortunately society often colludes in this delusion.

✦ ✦ ✦ Parasitic Nature

Another commonly observed characteristic of the sociopath is a parasitic nature. To someone targeted by a sociopath with strong parasitic tendencies it can feel quite literally as if the life is being sucked out of them. Parasitic behavior is associated with passive aggression.[2] Passive-aggressive individuals do not deal with things directly. They talk behind your back and put others in the position of telling you what they will not say themselves. They find subtle ways of letting you know they are unhappy. They are unlikely to show their anger or resentment. Instead, they conceal it behind a façade of affability, politeness, and well-meaning. However, underneath there is usually manipulation going on.

Types of passive aggression include:

victimization—when a person is unable to look at his or her part in a situation and turns the tables to become the victim, or at least to behave like one

self-pity—the "poor me" scenario

blaming others for situations rather than being able to take responsibility for one's own actions

withholding—avoiding performing one's usual behaviors, roles, or responsibilities in order to reinforce one's anger to the other party

learned helplessness—when a person acts as if he cannot help himself, sometimes to the point of deliberately doing a poor job of something to make a point

The important thing to note is that passive aggression is a destructive pattern of behavior and a form of emotional abuse. Such behaviors cause great distress to the target, who often feels overburdened with guilt and responsibility.[3]

◆◆◆ Manipulative Behavior

Psychological manipulation is a mainstay of the sociopath, who uses behavior to influence or control others in a deceptive and dishonest way. Advancing the interests of the manipulator, often at another's expense, such methods are exploitative, abusive, devious, and deceptive.

Manipulators may control their victims through some combination of the following methods:

positive reinforcement—employing praise, superficial charm, superficial sympathy ("crocodile tears"), excessive apologies, money, approval, gifts, attention, and public displays of emotional responses, such as forced laughter, or facial expressions, such as smiling

negative reinforcement—removing a negative situation as a reward; for example, "You won't have to pay all those bills by yourself if you allow me to move in with you"

intermittent or partial reinforcement—when rules, rewards, or personal boundaries are inconsistently handed out or enforced; used to create a climate of fear and doubt punishment—including nagging, intimidation, threats, swearing, emotional blackmail, and crying (to play the victim)

A sociopathic manipulator can cause you to believe you are going crazy. If you find yourself in a relationship where you think you need to keep a record of what's been said and you begin to question your own sanity, it is likely you are experiencing emotional manipulation. A sociopath is an expert in turning things around, rationalizing, justifying, and explaining things away. He lies so smoothly and argues so persuasively that you begin to doubt your own senses. Over a period of time this can distort your sense of reality. The sociopath can make you feel guilty for speaking up or not speaking up, for being emotional or not being emotional enough, for caring or for not caring enough. Manipulation is a powerful strategy. Most of us are conditioned to check ourselves, and we are usually our own worst critics. If accused of being in the wrong or acting imperfectly, we do whatever is necessary to reduce our feelings of guilt.

Another powerful strategy of the sociopath is to demand sympathy. The sociopath plays the victim remarkably well. However, he seldom fights his own fights or does his own dirty work. In the last chapter James manipulated Sam's friends, first by encouraging a fellow student to start a whispering campaign, and then by feeding the hostilities that caused some of the young people to gang up and attack Sam. Manipulators also use verbal abuse, explosive anger, or other intimidating behaviors to establish dominance or superiority; even one incident of such behavior can condition or train the target to avoid upsetting, confronting, or contradicting the manipulator.[4]

According to psychologists Babiak and Hare, sociopaths are always on the lookout for individuals to scam or swindle. They outline the sociopathic approach as having three phases.[5]

1. The Assessment Phase

Some sociopaths will take advantage of almost anyone they meet, while others are more patient, waiting for the perfect innocent target to cross their path. In each case, the sociopath is sizing up the potential usefulness of an individual as a source of money, power, or influence. Some sociopaths enjoy a challenge, while others prey on people who are vulnerable. During the assessment phase, the sociopath determines a potential target's weak points and uses them to lead the target off course.

2. The Manipulation Phase

After identifying a target, the sociopath may create a persona or "mask" specifically designed to work for the target. A sociopath will lie to gain the trust of the target. Sociopaths' lack of empathy and guilt allows them to lie with impunity; they do not see the value of telling the truth unless it will help them get what they want. As the interaction with the target proceeds, the sociopath carefully assesses the target's traits and characteristics so she can exploit them. The sociopath may also manipulate the target into revealing insecurities or weaknesses the target wishes to hide from view.

Over time, the sociopath builds a personal relationship with the target based on this knowledge. The false persona of the sociopath—the "personality" the target is bonding with—does not really exist. It is built on lies, carefully woven together to entrap the targeted person. It is a mask, one of many, customized to fit the target's particular expectations. This act of manipulation is predatory in nature and often leads to severe physical or emotional harm for the person targeted. Healthy relationships are built on mutual respect and trust; the targeted person believes mistakenly that the "bond" between himself and the sociopath is of that kind, and that this is why their relationship is so successful. When the sociopath behaves disrespectfully or breaches the target's trust, such incidents are overlooked.

3. The Abandonment Phase

This is when the sociopath decides that his target is no longer useful. He abandons the target and moves on to a new one. Sometimes, perhaps not surprisingly, targets overlap. The sociopath can "play" several individuals simultaneously: one who has just been abandoned but is kept in the picture in case the others do not work out; another who is currently being played; and a third who is being groomed in readiness.

♦ ♦ ♦ Pathological Lying

The fact is that sociopaths lie. There are two recognized categories of people who constantly lie: compulsive and pathological liars. The first—compulsive liars—lie out of habit. There is no real reason, and they normally don't lie to intentionally hurt anyone. The latter—pathological liars—lie for altogether different reasons. This category is the one into which sociopaths usually fall. Sociopathic liars lie to gain something. Their lying is often calculated and cunning. Sociopaths don't care whom their lies will affect, as long as the lie fits their purpose and achieves what they want. Unlike compulsive liars, sociopathic liars *can* help themselves. They may well know the difference between right and wrong, but the crux of the matter is they don't care—though they can be so good at lying that they believe their own lies.

Pathological lying is an invaluable tool for a sociopath, who uses it to gain pity and sympathy. If you pay very close attention you may catch a sociopath in a lie because she has a tendency to tell different versions of the same lie to different people. However, the sociopath is apt to make sure that individuals who have been told different stories don't have the chance to meet or compare stories. She may even keep friends and acquaintances apart to minimize the risk of being exposed. And if she is exposed, the sociopath doesn't balk at telling a new lie to cover the old. Always remember when dealing with a sociopath that lying doesn't worry her one bit. Your feelings don't matter. The sociopath doesn't have the capability or desire to care about you. Nobody is "special" to a sociopath unless they're serving her a purpose.

Sociopaths are highly likely to lie about their credentials; for example, when applying for a job a sociopath might well fake his resume. Don't be surprised if you find out that your sociopathic boss never earned a degree, let alone graduated from an Ivy League school, as was stated on his resume. Sociopaths are also likely to lie about previous relationships. Teenage sociopaths are likely to lie about situational circumstances. James, the school bully, lied to other people about the situation that Sam faced at home and was covert in his efforts to bring Sam down. He also had no qualms about making up accusations that a teacher was violent toward a pupil. Sociopaths are likely to falsely accuse another person of physical or mental abuse, especially if it will help them in a divorce or custody situation.

Pathological lying is persistent lying. It doesn't matter if the lies are easily disproved, because for some illogical reason they are seldom challenged. The lies sociopaths create may be fantastic in nature, extensive, elaborate, and complicated. Often there is a blurring between fiction and reality. The magnitude of the lie or its callous nature is irrelevant, and so are any consequences. Such characteristics have led researchers to conclude that the lying behavior might be gratifying in itself, and the expected reward external.

Not all sociopaths necessarily lie about factual things, but they are almost always unreliable or untrustworthy in one way or another.[6]

♦ ♦ ♦ Faking Illness

A lot of sociopaths lie about being ill or about being in recovery from a serious illness. They exaggerate or create symptoms to gain attention, evoke sympathy, or seek financial gain. No matter how bad your situation, the sociopath has experienced it ten times worse. This behavior is a form of hypochondriasis, though it is unlikely that the sociopath actually believes he has a disease. It is common for sociopaths to feign serious illnesses, rare conditions, or life-threatening diseases like cancer. Whatever the goal, the basis of the behavior is to seek advantage and personal profit. This was probably the driving force behind James's frequent fake illnesses. Feigning illness was also a habit of Rebecca's sociopathic mother. Her frequent illnesses and obsessive behaviors were tactics designed to gain attention and sympathy from her husband and to get more control at home.

♦ ♦ ♦ Aggression and Antisocial Behavior

When a sociopath is sad or angry everyone knows it, for she can fly into terrible rages. Sociopaths exhibit anger or attempt to gain your pity when they're intent on deceiving you. They rely on the fact that your judgment will be affected by your conscience and feelings of guilt if you don't respond to the situation sensitively or fairly.

Our case studies describe many examples of antisocial behavior, most of which were dressed up as something else by the expert manipulators we portrayed. James, an expert covert aggressive, was a master of the clandestine maneuver. His ability to tell lies was matched by his convincing ability to feign outrage. His most remarkable feat was his allegation of physical assault against the teacher. Such overt displays of emotion, while fake, often persuade outsiders to accept the sociopath's view of events. Manipulation must occur for us not to see the aggression and antisocial behavior for what it is. The sociopath's methods obscure our view so that she or he can "get away with murder," as it were. This is how Rebecca's mother managed to physically and emotionally torment her daughter while keeping her behavior hidden from her husband.

The sociopath's reliance on bullying and sabotage frequently also reveals itself in the workplace. John, the workplace sociopath, was very competitive. Although competitiveness is a common trait in sociopaths, it is also commonplace in society. The worlds of school and work in effect promote it, and nowhere is this more apparent than in business and politics. In our story John is not just competitive, however; he is covertly aggressive to others. He shows vindictiveness toward other humans and extreme cruelty to his dog. Cruelty to animals is thought to be common among sociopaths. Nevertheless, sociopaths are likely to use pets as props to convince a new target of their kindheartedness and trustworthiness.

Another pattern of sociopathic aggression is child-on-child cruelty. A real-life case is the death of little Jamie Bulger, a toddler murdered by two ten-year-old boys in Liverpool, England, in 1993. That two ten-year-olds could commit such a heinous crime was received with disbelief. So was the 2009 case of fifteen-year-old Alyssa Bustamante, of Missouri, who killed her nine-year-old neighbor Elizabeth Olten because she "wanted to know what it felt like" to kill someone. These cases show that sociopathic children do exist, even if the word "sociopath" is never mentioned in the reporting of their stories. Sociopathy is so far removed from our understanding of what it is to be young and human, it seems, that we refuse to acknowledge the condition in minors.

◆ ◆ ◆ Lack of Empathy and Remorse

Simon Baron-Cohen, author of *Zero Degrees of Empathy*, defines empathy as an ability to identify what someone else is thinking or feeling, and to respond to their thoughts and feelings with an appropriate emotion.[7] What causes people to be capable of seriously hurting one another is not rightly understood, but when our empathy is "switched off" and we operate solely on an "I" basis (viewing the world as if we were the only ones who exist or matter), we are much more inclined to regard other people as objects. This is thought to be the viewpoint held by sociopaths.

of "teacher" was given a list of word pairs that he was to teach the "learner." The teacher was then given an electric shock from an electroshock generator as a sample of the shock that the learner would supposedly receive in response to wrong answers.

The teacher began the experiment by reading the list to the learner. The teacher then read the first word of each pair and read four possible answers. The learner was asked to press a button to indicate his response. If the answer was incorrect, the teacher would administer a shock to the learner, with the voltage increasing incrementally for each wrong answer. If the learner's answer was correct, the teacher would read the next word pair. The subjects believed that for each wrong answer, the learner was receiving an actual shock. In fact, there were no shocks.

During the experiment, many people indicated their desire to stop and check on the learner, and some paused to question the purpose of the experiment. But most continued after being assured that they wouldn't be held responsible. A few subjects began to laugh nervously or exhibit other signs of extreme stress after hearing staged screams of pain coming from the learner. If the subject indicated that he wanted to halt the experiment, he was given verbal instructions by the experimenter, in this order:

Please continue.
The experiment requires that you continue.
It is absolutely essential that you continue.
You have no other choice, you must go on.

If the subject still wished to stop after hearing all four instructions, the experiment was halted. Otherwise, it was stopped after the learner had (supposedly) been given the maximum 450-volt shock three times in succession. In the experiments, 62.5 percent of the "teachers" administered the experiment's final, massive 450-volt shock, though many were very uncomfortable doing so.

Afterward, Milgram summarized the experiment in an article for *Harper's* titled "The Perils of Obedience":

Ordinary people, simply doing their jobs, and without any particular hostility on their part, can become agents in a terrible destructive process.

Moreover, even when the destructive effects of their work become patently clear and they are asked to carry out actions incompatible with fundamental standards of morality, relatively few people have the resources needed to resist authority.[1]

Milgram's experiments have been repeated many times, yielding consistent results. What this evidence suggests is that a person of authority can strongly influence other people's behavior. This is relatively useful in one way, as it makes it easy for an authority such as a government to establish order and control. But in the wrong hands such power and influence can have catastrophic consequences. The dubious nature of Milgram's experiments has attracted a great deal of ethical criticism, most importantly that he deceived the participants and didn't take adequate measures to protect them—indeed, within the context of this book, you might be forgiven for thinking such rather callous experiments have sociopathic tendencies. (Milgram's defense was that the results were unexpected and that their surprising nature, as much as the methods he used, may have evoked the criticisms.)

Apaths are portrayed in the 2008 film *The Wave*, by German writer, actor, and director Dennis Gansel, in which high-school teacher Rainer Wenger sets out to examine the issue of autocracy. His students, the third generation after the Second World War, don't believe that a dictatorship could be established in modern Germany, so Wenger starts an experiment to demonstrate how easily the masses can be manipulated, rearranging the class on fascistic principles that include adopting a uniform, devising a salute, and excluding nonconformists. Most of the students follow the new rules (i.e., they are apaths—people who blindly adhere to authority).

One student, Mona, however, leaves the group in disgust (in our view of things she is an empath, a category we will discuss next). The other classmates do not see any connection between their activity and fascism; they believe that only good things have come from the movement. One young man, Tim (from our perspective an apath), becomes strongly committed to the group, offering to become Wenger's bodyguard. Wenger whips up the students' fervor as they continue to go along wholeheartedly with the new situation, but he finally insists that the experiment must end and sends everyone home. Tim produces a pistol and demands that everyone stay. He is desperate for the new arrangement to continue because it has become his life. One of the other boys approaches Tim, who shoots him before turning the gun on himself.[2]

This film, based on the book of the same name, was inspired by a real-life social experiment called the Third Wave, one of a number of studies that examined the disabling of conscience and humans' tendency to adhere blindly to authority. The experiment was conducted in 1967 by teacher Ron Jones at Cubberley High School, in Palo Alto, California. It was designed to demonstrate that democratic societies are not immune to the appeal of fascism.[3]

What this experiment and film demonstrate is that some people are more malleable than others. Importantly, they show us that a greater number of individuals lack a backbone than perhaps we would like to think. In fact, studies suggest that over 60 percent of us have a tendency to "follow the leader," whether that leader is malign or benign. Within this majority group lurk the apaths, the foot soldiers of the sociopath. Apaths are less able to see a situation for what it really is; their view of the bigger picture is obscured by their attitude toward and opinion of the target, and by the sociopath's mesmeric influence.

Apaths are often fearful individuals who feel they do not possess the skill required to confront a challenge. They are the ones most likely to go with the flow, to agree that the emperor is wearing new clothes. But apaths may also fail to perceive any threat at all. A danger is of no importance if one denies its existence. An apath's response to a sociopath's call to arms can result from a state of "learned helplessness." Apaths behave defenselessly because they want to avoid unpleasant or harmful circumstances. Apathy is an avoidance strategy.

To shed more light on the behavior of apaths we'll relate some real-life stories. The first account comes from Nancy Ellen, who survived life with a sociopathic mother and was left to face difficult times because of her father's inaction:

> My father was one of seven brothers. My mother was one of fourteen children. Not one relative ever went out of their way to try to help me or even invite me to play with my cousins. Growing up I was very isolated because we didn't participate in holiday gatherings with any relatives. My mother always had a sour attitude and complained about everyone. No

one visited us, and I was trapped in my childhood hell with a sociopathic mother and a loving father who worked all the time (partly to avoid having to be around his wife). I felt like an outcast from a very young age.

My father was a World War II veteran who had spent four years in France, Germany, and Austria. His troop liberated the Dachau concentration camp. Post-traumatic stress disorder, or PTSD, was unknown in those days, but I would say that my father had PTSD, triggered by the many atrocities he saw. I think the combination of his childhood, with a stern and possibly abusive Italian immigrant father, and the war meant that what emotions he experienced were held deep inside. I only saw my father cry twice in my life, when a good friend died and when he himself was dying. Whenever I sought his help about my sociopathic mother, he would tell me to ignore her and not pay her any attention because she was nuts like the rest of her family.

As a teenager, once I had a car, my father would give me money for gas and would tell me, "Go out with your friends and get away from her." He never divorced my mother because he didn't want to split his assets with her. By not getting a divorce, he left me with a mess, because eventually, after he died, the money he intended for me to inherit was stolen from me by a maternal cousin. I would say he felt helpless about the situation. I know they didn't divorce when I was younger because he didn't want my mother to use me as a pawn, and he felt that leaving me with her 100 percent of the time would be detrimental to my well-being.

I know he did the best he could, and I am not mad at my father at all. I don't know how he put up with my mother. I suppose he compensated for the situation at home by working a lot and by supporting his family financially, which was his socially accepted role. Dad and his six brothers ran a large corporation. Five of my uncles' families are taken care of financially, but two of us have been cheated out of at least one million dollars. My father did buy a house for me to live in with my little boy after I got divorced. He bought a house for himself, too, because he couldn't tolerate his sociopathic wife any longer. He was a solitary man who sought peace and quiet in his retirement years away from his wife.

When my inheritance was stolen by my maternal cousin, I sought out a couple of my maternal aunts and uncles, and they did nothing. I sought out a couple of paternal cousins, but they did nothing. One cousin said he would pray for me. They didn't have their inheritance stolen. The toll of the abuse—both emotional and financial—has been harsh.

Another survivor of childhood sociopathic abuse is Colleen, who experienced physical and emotional abuse at the hands of her mother. What compounded her unhappiness at home was her father's apparent inability to deal with the abuse. Here she discusses her father's apathy and some possible reasons for it:

My father was the eldest son of seven children. He grew up poor, as did many Afrikaners, having lost all their land in the Boer War. He only got an education by winning scholarships. He went to fight in the Second World War against his parents' wishes (his own father had been in a British concentration camp as a very small child and had lost a brother and a sister there), and he never really recovered from the experience. He was a pilot during the war, and suffered depression all his life from things he saw. He had a breakdown and spent a month or two in the hospital, which is when my mother started taking lovers. Later he worked in the British diplomatic corps.

I always worshipped my father. To me, he was "The Good One." He didn't spend much time with me, but what time he did spend I treasured. He made me a beautiful dollhouse with real windows and a staircase (I watched closely and later made one for my own children, albeit out of cardboard). He took me sailing, and we would go on long walks and drives, just exploring the countryside while doing things like searching for the source of a river.

When my mother was nasty to me, he would take me aside and explain that she hadn't been loved as a child, and that she didn't mean to hurt me, and really loved me, and that we must be very kind and understanding toward her. I only realized much later how harmful that was; it really set me up for my narcissistic husband! Even as recently as a year ago, it dawned on me that although my father took me sailing, he didn't have me wear a life jacket. And I was allowed to sit right out on the prow. He took risks with my safety. One New Year's Eve, as we stood out in the snow on the large balcony of our apartment, he put a firecracker in my hand. I remember my mother protesting, but he said it was safe—it said so on the packet. He lit it, and a few seconds later it exploded in my hand.

I nearly lost two fingers. I was rushed to a hospital that specialized in burns, where I spent a couple of weeks being spoiled rotten by the staff. So although I loved my father, I couldn't really trust his judgment.

Later he developed a drinking problem, and then life became really complicated. My father let me down badly in the end. For many years he told me how I'd never have to worry about my children because he'd created an education fund for them. There was no such thing.

Turning a blind eye is a common trait of the apath, as the following story also makes evident. George was so used to his sociopathic wife's telling him what to do and what to say that he didn't see anything wrong with it. He learned to act defenselessly as a means of getting through life. It became more or less a habit to turn a blind eye if his wife challenged or threatened others, even if the person targeted happened to be one of their children. George's wife bossed him around in order to keep control of her domain and possessions—which included family members, whom she viewed as objects, not human beings.

If she felt someone was getting too close to her foot-soldier husband, she would view them as a threat and start an offensive. Her usual approach was to slyly make snide remarks and hurtful comments about the person, or to tell lies about his or her character. If the victim responded angrily, as naturally most would, she would turn to her husband and say, "See, George, I told you, she hates me." George would go along, lending support to her outrage. It is likely that he occasionally overheard the criticisms and accusations she directed at the targeted person but chose to ignore them. And she, accustomed to his passivity, had long ceased bothering to keep her remarks out of earshot. In the end he became so practiced in self-trickery and so fearful of a showdown that he submissively went along with her every time.

In the case histories presented in Chapter 1, we saw similar behavior exhibited by Rebecca's loving but dispirited father, and we saw Susan, the downtrodden wife of Peter, adopt the apath role during the worst years of her marriage.

The Empath

Not always, but quite often, the person targeted by the sociopath is an empath. To understand why this happens, and what is going on when it happens, we first need to understand the definition of an empath. Most humans have the ability to empathize, but some have more ability than others. Empathy is a vague and elusive concept. For neuroscientist Jean Decety, empathy resembles "a sort of minor constellation…stars glowing in the cosmos of an otherwise dark brain." He is referring to the network of regions of the brain—the anterior cingulate cortex and anterior insula—that light up orange on an fMRI scan when a person witnesses another in pain.[4] Yet empathy is more than orange-lit parts of the brain. It is something that makes us human, or, rather, humane.

Empathy is a shared emotion. To show empathy is to put yourself emotionally in the place of another. It is a phenomenon that requires emotional control and the capacity to distinguish oneself from others. Most of us possess the automatic ability to perceive and share others' feelings. A baby listening to another baby cry may cry, too. People often unconsciously mimic the facial expressions of those they see. The ability to empathize is directly dependent on your ability to feel your own feelings and identify what they are. If you have never felt a certain feeling, it will be hard for you to understand how someone else is experiencing that feeling.

An empath, in the context in which we apply the term, is not a person with near magical powers such as mind reading. Empaths are ordinary people who are highly perceptive and insightful and belong to the estimated 40 percent of human beings who sense when something's not right (those who respond to their "gut instinct'). Going back to the folktale "The Emperor's New Clothes," the empath is the boy who mentions the unmentionable: that the emperor isn't wearing any clothes.

Back in the 1990s researchers suggested that there was a positive relationship between empathy and emotional intelligence.[5] Since then that term has been used interchangeably with "emotional literacy." What this means in practice is that empaths have the ability to understand their own emotions, to listen to other people and empathize with their emotions, to express emotions productively, and to handle their emotions in such a way as to improve their personal power.[6]

Empathy is a powerful communication tool that is often underused and undervalued in today's world. Yet the world needs as many empaths as it can find, for empaths are often mediators, go-betweens, and peacemakers.

Disharmony creates an uncomfortable feeling in an empath, and in a confrontation he will try to settle things quickly. People are often attracted to empaths because of their compassionate nature. Even complete strangers find it easy to talk to empaths about personal matters because in general they make great listeners. A particular attribute of empaths is that they are sensitive to the emotional distress of others. Conversely they have trouble comprehending a closed mind or a lack of compassion in others. They can be highly expressive and inclined to talk openly about themselves, although they often find it difficult to handle a compliment. Very highly empathetic people (sometimes termed super-empaths) may find themselves helping others at the expense of their own needs, which can lead them to withdraw from the outside world and become loners.

It's odd: most of us enjoy watching films and reading books about heroes who refuse to go along with the crowd, which suggests there is something admirable about people who make a bold stand, but in real life watching someone raise their head above the parapet often makes the rest of us feel queasy. Most—a majority of 60-plus percent—prefer the easy life and choose to maintain the status quo. What prevents many of us from acting on our consciences is fear; fear hems us in. It was interesting to discover, when doing the research for this book, how often people referred to empathetic types as fearful, too sensitive, and vulnerable. In other words, many see empaths in problematic terms. It is true that some psychologists consider super-empathy a personality disorder or difficulty in its own right, especially if an individual reaches a state where he is so moved by others' emotions that he is overwhelmed by the amount of empathy he feels. But our experience suggests that people of such extreme empathy are few and far between. At any rate most empaths thrive very well in spite of, or indeed because of, their easy ability to empathize.

Empaths use their ability to empathize to boost their and others' well-being and safety. Problems can arise for empaths, however, whenever there are apaths in the vicinity. Empaths can be brought down, distressed, and forced into the position of the lone fighter by the inaction of more apathetic types around them. Here is a typical scenario involving an empath named Cameron who is fighting unaided among apaths:

Cameron spied a boy being bullied by a gang behind the baseball field. Other boys must have witnessed the incident, as he saw several of them walking close by. Without hesitation Cameron shouted to the gang to stop kicking the boy. Cameron's friends, who had been laughing and poking fun at each other moments before, watched aghast and then one by one began to creep away from the scene. Suddenly the field was deserted and Cameron faced the gang alone. He couldn't walk away and leave the boy to get a beating; his conscience would not allow it. So he braved their insults and name-calling and stood there, determined not to back down. The gang leader sensed that his authority was weakened by Cameron's presence, so he told the others to let go of the victim. "We'll get him later," he said, "when this ****'s not around to spoil things." To Cameron's surprise and disappointment, when the boy was released from the gang's clutches, he was less than grateful that he had missed out on a beating. Cameron didn't know what infuriated him more: the boy's lack of gratitude or the fact that his friends were nowhere to be seen.

The Sociopathic Transaction

Often empaths are targeted by sociopaths because they pose the greatest threat. The empath is usually the first to detect that something is not right and to express what he or she senses. As a consequence, the empath is both the sociopath's number-one foe and a source of attraction; the empath's responses and actions provide excellent entertainment for a bored and listless sociopath going about her daily business. Cameron's story highlights what happens to empaths who become embroiled in the actions of a bully.

The world of the empath is not for the fainthearted, and it is easy to see why others walk away from these kinds of confrontational situations. In the context that we are discussing, empaths often find themselves up against not only the sociopath but quite often a flock of apaths as well. Apaths hide among the 60 percent of people who obediently follow the leader. On the basis of these traits they are afforded pole position in the sociopath's intrigues. But this prime spot comes at a price, for in what we call the sociopathic transaction, the apath makes an unspoken Faustian pact with the sociopath, and then passively (often through fear) or otherwise participates in his cruel sport.

The Sociopath-Empath-Apath Triad (SEAT)

For a sociopathic transaction to be effective it requires the following three-some: a sociopath, an empath, and an apath. We call this the Sociopath-Empath-Apath Triad—SEAT for short. The usual setup goes something like this: On seeing the sociopath say or do something underhanded, the empath is forced to make a stand. The empath challenges the sociopath, who throws others off the scent by shifting the blame to the empath. The empath becomes an object of abuse when the apath corroborates the sociopath's perspective. Ultimately the situation usually ends badly for the empath, and sometimes also for the apath (if his conscience comes back to haunt him or subsequently he becomes an object of abuse himself). Frustratingly, however, the sociopath often gets off scot free.

Sociopaths rarely vary this tested formula because it virtually guarantees them success. In fact, in almost every sociopathic interaction we know of, this specific exchange is enacted. The sociopathic transaction relies heavily on the apathy of those close to the event or situation and highlights the importance of the apath in the transaction, as indicated in Figure 1.

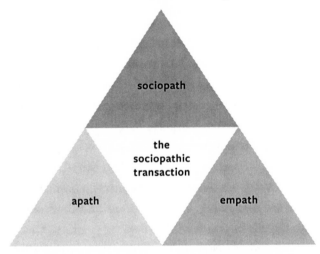

FIGURE 1. The Sociopath-Empath-Apath Triad (SEAT)

Sociopaths draw in apaths by numerous means: flattery, bribery, disorienting them with lies. A sociopath will go to any lengths to win her game. The best way to illustrate the interplay and the ease with which apaths are pulled in is through the story of Steve and Robin:

Steve and Robin were microbiologists at a prestigious university who were collaborating on an important vaccine trial. The department chair, Ben, was the principal investigator. An arrogant and surly man in his early forties, Ben was a taskmaster and a bully, though lauded by the university bigwigs because his reputation for excellent research helped secure large grants. With this new project he hoped to gain substantially; an important new vaccine could see his status in his field rise still further and prove the catalyst for a glittering scientific career.

His colleagues worked relentlessly collecting data. With the early phase over, Ben set about drafting a paper on their preliminary findings for submission to a respected scientific journal. Unbeknownst to his colleagues, Ben decided that the outcome didn't look nearly as tantalizing as he had hoped, so he falsified some key results in order to present their findings in the best possible light. On completing the first draft he sent out the paper for comment to his colleagues. Steve replied immediately by e-mail and confirmed he was happy with the manuscript. In fact he used the opportunity to suck up to his boss, thanking him for writing the paper so swiftly. Robin, on the other hand, was aghast. He read it over and over, noting what he saw as colossal errors. With great urgency, he rattled off an e-mail to Ben.

Receiving no immediate response, he phoned Ben. When Ben didn't pick up, Robin went to find him in person and discovered him in the cafeteria with Steve. He was already too late, however. Ben had poisoned Steve's mind, saying that Robin had challenged him over the accuracy of the results due to a long-standing grudge rooted in his own inefficiency. Ben told Steve that he had had to confront Robin about his own work several months back. Steve, however, was different, Ben implied—much more thorough. He intimated that Steve would be on course for promotion, "especially if we get this paper out and secure funding for the next-stage trials." By the time Robin joined them, Steve, though initially shocked, had already been won over by Ben's swift flattery and insinuations.

Seeing Ben and Steve together, Robin crossed the cafeteria to them. "Hi, you two got a moment?" There was an awkward silence. Steve exchanged a look with Ben, who gave a slight conspiratorial smile. "Yes, we've got a few moments. We were just talking about the paper. By the way, I did see your e-mail, but if you look at the paper thoroughly I think you'll find that everything is correct." Robin turned to Steve to see how he was reacting to this charade. Steve looked at him smugly. "I'm with Ben on this one, Robin. There are no flaws in the analysis or the write-up of the study that I can see. We should be grateful Ben got it turned around so quickly."

Robin was totally floored. "You can't be serious. You're happy for it to go off to be reviewed with all these serious errors in it? Our reputations will be left in ruins when this gets out." Robin decided to make a stand. He asked for his name to be removed as a coauthor of the paper but was exasperated to learn that it was sent off to the journal anyway. More frustratingly still, it was published within a few months. Meanwhile, the workplace became a source of stress for Robin as he struggled to cope with the backlash from colleagues who saw his intervention as an attempt to sabotage their work. People avoided him at break times, and when they did talk to him the conversation was awkward and stilted.

Eventually Robin arranged a meeting with Ben to have it out once and for all. But when the time came for the meeting Ben took control of the agenda. "Robin, I have to be honest with you, many of your colleagues are unhappy about the way you handled things, and some have made complaints about the standard of your recent work. Furthermore, your colleagues don't trust you to conduct yourself professionally after you attempted to sabotage their hard work. Mercifully the reviewers saw what a damn fine trial we'd conducted and didn't get wind of your attempted slur. We can't afford to have a saboteur on the team, someone so reckless they would put the whole research project at risk. So I've discussed this with the dean, and he agrees there's no future for you here and no other way to deal with this. You've got to go."

The "Gaslighting" Effect

Let's take a look at the sociopath's standard mode of operation. According to Martha Stout, sociopaths frequently use what are called "gaslighting" tactics. In our story, Ben (the sociopath) targets Robin (the empath) and uses Steve (the apath) as a corroborator in the abuse. The actions of both Ben and Steve have a gaslighting effect on Robin.

Gaslighting is the systematic attempt by one person to erode another's reality. The syndrome gets its name from the 1938 British stage play *Gas Light* (originally known as *Angel Street* in the United States), and from the 1940 and 1944 film adaptations. The 1944 film *Gaslight* features a murderer who attempts to make his wife doubt her sanity. He uses a variety of tricks to convince her that she is crazy so she won't be believed when she reports the strange things that are genuinely occurring, including the dimming of the gas lamps in the house (which happens when her husband turns on the normally unused gas lamps in the attic to conduct clandestine activities there). The term has since found its way into clinical and research literature.

Gaslighting is a form of psychological abuse in which false information is presented in such a way as to make the target doubt his or her own memory and perception. Psychologists call this, rather incongruously, "the sociopath's dance." It may simply involve the denial by an abuser that previous abusive incidents ever occurred, or it could be the staging of strange events intended to disorientate the target. In any event, the effect of gaslighting is to arouse such an extreme sense of anxiety and confusion in the target that he reaches the point where he no longer trusts his own judgment. The techniques are similar to those used in brainwashing, interrogation, and torture—the instruments of psychological warfare. This is Machiavellian behavior of the worst kind. A target exposed to it for long enough loses her sense of self. She finds herself second-guessing her memory; she becomes depressed and withdrawn and totally dependent on the abuser for her sense of reality. The endgame for the sociopath (or gaslighter) is when the target (or gaslightee, often an empath) thinks he is going crazy.

Anyone can become the victim of a sociopath's gaslighting moves. Gaslighting can take place in any kind of relationship—between parent and child, or between siblings, friends, or work colleagues. Going back to our analogy of the emperor's new clothes, it is the process of gaslighting that distorts our sense of reality and makes us disbelieve what we see. Even when the victim is bewildered, there is a reluctance on his or her part to see the gaslighter for what he is. Denial is essential for gaslighting to work.

Psychotherapist Christine Louis de Canonville describes different phases through which the abuser leads the relationship: the idealization stage, the devaluation stage, and the discarding stage.[7] Gaslighting does not happen all at once, so if you suspect in the early stages of a relationship that you are being gaslighted, you can protect yourself by walking away. However, you need to be informed as to what the stages look like to make that choice. Let's explore them briefly.

◆◆◆The Idealization Stage

During this early stage the sociopath shows herself in the best possible light. But this phase is an illusion. The sociopath intends only to draw her target in. At the beginning of the relationship she is usually ultra-attentive, charming, energetic, exciting, and great fun. If the context is a new romantic relationship, the targeted person may feel he loves the sociopath intensely. It can feel like an addictive or hypnotic sort of love. Caught up in the euphoria, he becomes hooked. If the context is a friendship, the person targeted may feel she has never in her life met anyone with whom she has more in common. In the workplace, the person may feel he has finally found a boss who sees his true potential. The target does all he can to gain the sociopath's special approval. The boss might tempt him along with words to the effect of "I see a lot of me in you."

◆◆◆The Devaluation Stage

Once the sociopath has assessed the target's strengths and weaknesses, the first phase is over and the devaluation stage begins. From here on in, the sociopath is cold and unfeeling. This phase begins gradually so the targeted person is not alert to the transformation. Nevertheless, at some point it will begin to seem to the target that she can't do anything right. She feels devalued at every turn. Totally confused, the targeted person becomes increasingly stressed, unhappy, low in mood, or depressed. The gaslighting effect is under way. Confused by the sociopath's behavior, the targeted person tries harder to please her abuser in order to get the relationship back on track. But no matter what she does she only seems to cause the sociopath further injury. The target gets caught up in a spiral of sociopathic abuse where unpredictability and uncertainty are routine, until finally she becomes a shadow of her former self. The paradox of the situation is that the more distressed the target becomes, the more the sociopath enjoys the power of the situation, and the more powerful the sociopath feels, the more blatant and extreme his abuse becomes.

Devaluation, according to Louis de Canonville, can be delivered through many different forms and levels of attack. The targeted person has been conditioned, appearing to the outside world to be a willing partner in the sociopath's games. If she does manage to escape the sociopathic individual, she is at high risk of future entrapment by other sociopaths, because she is primed in a way that other sociopaths can spot.

◆◆◆The Discarding Stage

In the discarding stage, the game comes to its conclusion. By this time the sociopath has lost her ardor for the game, for she views the contest as already won. The target is reduced to an object, something to which the sociopath is totally indifferent; it is as if the targeted individual no longer exists. The targeted person, on the other hand, is left confused and raw with emotion. In the context of a romantic association he may scramble to find a way to rescue the dying relationship. But the sociopath resists all attempts to reestablish any connection, using bullying tactics such as silence or coldness in retaliation; she is probably already making moves to secure her next target.

◆◆◆The Relentless Pursuit

Sometimes, instead of discarding the targeted person, the abuser will refuse to let her leave the relationship. (This dynamic isn't described in the model proposed by Louis de Canonville.) The sociopath can't take no for an answer and will continually attempt to make contact with the target, perhaps even in violation of a restraining order. This especially seems to be a pattern among men who are domestic abusers. According to some experts, the life and physical safety of a battered woman are in the greatest danger *after* she has left her violent partner.

The Effects of Gaslighting from the Targeted Person's Point of View

During the process of gaslighting, the targeted person usually goes through certain recognizable emotional and psychological states. Psychologist Robin Stern describes three stages gaslightees experience: disbelief, defense, and depression.[8]

✦ ✦ ✦ Disbelief

The targeted person's initial reaction to gaslighting behavior is one of complete disbelief; he cannot fathom the sudden change toward him, or that he is being gaslighted. All he knows is that something terribly distressing seems to be happening, but he can't figure out what. Blinded by the sociopath's promises or affections, the targeted person naturally trusts that his friendship or love is returned, but, of course, this belief is based on falsehood. In consequence, the sociopath offers no sympathy or support when the target seeks to put the relationship right.

Gaslighting doesn't need to be severe in order to have stark effects on the gaslighted person. It can be as subtle as being told, "You are so sensitive," or having it suggested that you are incapable: for example, "You can't do that. You'll have to leave it to me." Even though the targeted person knows on a rational level that these statements are untrue, his confidence is so eroded that he can't trust his own view. In extreme cases, those desperate for reassurance that they're not going mad become very dependent on their abuser for a sense of reality.

✦ ✦ ✦ Defense

In the early stages of the devaluation phase the targeted person still has the emotional wherewithal to defend himself against the manipulation. However, at some point he is thrown off balance by creeping self-doubt, anxiety, and guilt. Becoming bewildered and unable to trust his own instincts or memory, he tends to isolate himself because of the shame he feels. Eventually he is left unable to defend himself from the unbearable gaslighting effect.

One psychological condition that can result is called Stockholm syndrome. This got its name from a 1973 bank robbery in Stockholm, Sweden, in which four bank employees were strapped in dynamite and locked in a vault. Much to their rescuers' surprises, the hostages had developed more trust in their captors than in the police who were trying to rescue them. The term was subsequently coined by Swedish psychiatrist and criminologist Nils Bejerot, who was involved in the case.

Stockholm syndrome can occur in situations where people find themselves held captive and in fear of their lives—not only in kidnapping and hostage situations but also as a result of sociopathic abuse. It refers to the way in which a victim of the abuse may bond with his or her captor as a defense mechanism—a phenomenon technically known as traumatic bonding. In order to cope with the discomfort of living in such madness and chaos and to reduce the conflict they are experiencing, the targeted person—and the apath, too, if they are involved long enough—cope by rationalizing and excusing the sociopath's behavior. Christine Louis de Canonville calls it a "clever but complicated[,] unconscious" self-preservation strategy.

♦ ♦ ♦ Depression

By the time someone has been systematically gaslighted, he hardly recognizes himself. In fact, many such people become shadows of their former selves. They begin to feel that they can't do anything right anymore or that they can't trust their own mind or the opinion of others. So they withdraw and adopt a distorted perspective of what is really taking place. Some escape into a state of constant low mood or depression. Depression is different from normal sadness; it is worse, as it affects the person's physical health and lasts longer. A lot of people who have been gaslighted for a sustained period eventually experience post-traumatic stress disorder (see Chapter 4 for more on this topic). This is especially true of children of sociopathic parents.

In the aftermath of sociopathic abuse people may experience an array of responses: shock, disbelief, deep sadness, guilt, shame, anger, fear, loneliness, and anxious thoughts, as well as physical symptoms including panic attacks, flashbacks, fatigue, and dissociation. Many also express relief at finally knowing what has been going on. Confidence erosion is another symptom that follows gaslighting. Gaslighted individuals live in fear of doing the wrong thing and making their situation even more dangerous or unpleasant. They become more cautious and doubt themselves. This often affects how they make decisions. They commonly ask, "Am I too sensitive?" "Why do I attract people like this?" "Am I to blame?" Shame and blame are hallmarks of gaslighting. The targeted person may become hypersensitive after constant humiliation. He hears countless times from the sociopath and her foot-soldier apaths that he is "too sensitive," so over time he begins to believe these lies about himself.

Another negative side effect of having been gaslighted is that the targeted person finds herself always apologizing, even for her very existence. This is a way of avoiding more conflict with the sociopath, and many children of sociopathic parents have a tendency to do it. It is not an act of politeness. Rather, as Christine Louis de Canonville argues, it is a powerful strategy for staying safe and a means of disarming the sociopath.

One more effect of gaslighting on the targeted person is joylessness, a melancholic view of life. Many people who have experienced the traumatic effects of gaslighting go through such physical and mental tortures that they suffer a personality change. They may end up feeling confused, lonely, frightened, and unhappy. But rather than expose their vulnerability they hold on to it and keep their feelings in. Targeted individuals often experience great shame about their situation. When well-meaning friends and family members show concern or ask whether they are okay, they avoid the topic and withhold information in order to shield themselves from further pain.

Shame resulting from sociopathic abuse is a difficult issue, and one we discuss in greater depth in the next chapter. The shame that a targeted person feels is a normal response to the sense of failure she suffers as a result of her inability to protect herself (and possibly her dependents) from abuse. In addition, other people often have a "blame the victim" mentality or take the attitude that the targeted person should "just get over it," both of which demoralize the individual concerned. This shame can be interpreted by others as defensiveness, but in reality it is likely that the individual wishes to withdraw and socially isolate herself out of fear and lack of trust of others.

Some people who have been gaslighted also experience difficulty in making simple decisions. Having to ask permission to do anything, not being allowed to express their own opinion, never being able to win an argument, constantly being chastised and humiliated—all of these dynamics contribute to a loss of their autonomy, even their ability to make decisions for themselves. Many individuals recovering from sociopathic abuse adopt "people pleasing" behavior as a way of coping and dealing with others. This occurs as a defense mechanism because the targeted person has become conditioned to attempting to please the sociopath. Sadly, the only person the targeted empath does not set out to please is himself.

The behavioral and emotional difficulties that follow abuse at the hands of a sociopath mean that, for the unfortunate few who have endured years of such abuse, life can seem rather hopeless. In Chapter 4 we will discuss strategies for coping with this aftermath and turning things around.

Coping in the Aftermath of a Destructive Relationship

When a sociopath performs his cruel play,
take your cue and exit the stage.
— Fin McGregor

THAT PEOPLE CAN SURVIVE sociopathic abuse is testament to the fortitude of the human spirit. In this chapter we will discuss what it takes to end interactions with a sociopath and get your life back.

Witnessing Sociopathic Abuse

What should you do if you are aware that sociopathic abuse is taking place? If your brush with a sociopath is only fleeting, or you have witnessed someone else being abused, you will probably feel inclined to immediately cease contact with the sociopath. But if you or someone else has been or remains in danger, you need to think about your obligation to report what you have experienced or witnessed to the police or other relevant agencies. In this way, you may prevent the same problem from happening again. Evidence from victims and witnesses is important because it demonstrates the distress and damage that sociopathic behavior can do in our communities. Apathy equates to collusion, so turning a blind eye is no option for a person of integrity.

Yet, in reality, many of us find it hard to get involved. One of the barriers to speaking out is that sociopaths often work on evoking other people's pity. You should never agree to help a sociopath conceal his or her true identity, whether out of pity or for any other reason. If you find yourself pitying someone who consistently hurts you or other people, and who actively seeks your sympathy, the chances are you are dealing with a sociopath. The best advice is not to listen. In *The Sociopath Next Door*, Martha Stout stresses that while there is still interaction between you and the sociopath, it is best to resist the temptation to join in his games.[1] Trying to outsmart the sociopath or getting into arguments with him reduces you to his level—and distracts you from the task of protecting yourself. It is better to resist a showdown with a sociopath at all costs. In such situations his drive to win sets in. The best way to protect yourself is to avoid him, and to refuse any kind of contact or communication. Sociopaths feel no obligation to you or anyone else. To keep a sociopath in your life is therefore to put yourself at risk of harm.

If you find it difficult to exclude the sociopath from your life, it might help to remind yourself that by doing so you won't hurt anyone's feelings. Sociopaths' emotional repertoire is so limited that they don't have feelings to hurt. So look at the situation dispassionately. If you find that your family, friends, and acquaintances have difficulty understanding why you want to avoid a particular individual, and they put unwanted pressure on you to continue the relationship, don't give in. Remain unmoved by those who don't comprehend the danger of the situation, and have the strength of your convictions.

If total avoidance is out of the question—for instance, if the sociopath is someone you work with—limit contact as much as possible. Above all, make the rules of engagement ones that are right for you, and then do your utmost to stick to them. View the boundaries on contact as nonnegotiable, and turn a deaf ear to those who ask for explanations. Conversely, don't be afraid to be unsmiling or serious when explaining your position.

At some point most of us learn that we can't control other people's behavior. This is important to keep at the forefront of your mind, as is the crucial point that the sociopath's behavior is not your fault. It is far better to concentrate on your own behavior and on sorting out your own life than to bother with things you can't change.

Dealing with the Draining Effects of Trauma

If you have been on the receiving end of direct and/or sustained sociopathic abuse, you may feel confused and bewildered in the aftermath. This section is intended to help you deal with the initial trauma and help you get back on your feet.

The very first steps toward recovery involve recognizing and accepting that abuse has occurred and taking steps to remove the sociopath from your life, or to severely limit her influence. Recognizing and accepting the abuser and the abuse for what they are is a vital first step. Doing so helps draw the issue to the surface and lets you see and make sense of what has been happening to you.

Next, seek out help and support for yourself. If talking openly and directly to someone like a professional counselor is too difficult at first, then "talking to oneself" is a pretty good start. Talking to oneself can include finding and reading useful self-help books, such as this one, and searching the Internet for online support groups and useful blogs (see Resources). Online groups can provide instant support and advice, as well as the chance to begin incorporating a new and stronger voice into your real-life identity over time. Online groups also provide a level of anonymity, though it is important to protect your privacy, especially if you are feeling especially vulnerable and at a crisis point in your life. So a word or two of caution about use of the Internet: Only discuss things you are willing to share and to leave available in the public domain. Many online groups, such as those on Facebook, have privacy policies and other policies in place to regulate proceedings, but sociopaths and other antisocial types love to lurk online, manifesting themselves as Internet "trolls" (people who post inflammatory or insulting messages in an online community such as a forum, chat room, or blog). The message to heed is this: Keep your wits about you, trust and respond to your gut instincts, and proceed with caution.

Identifying any problems you are experiencing that have resulted from your interactions with a sociopath can seem a mammoth task at first. As discussed, in the aftermath of sociopathic abuse individuals can feel such an extreme sense of anxiety and confusion that they no longer trust their own judgment. Entering a sociopathic relationship is a one-sided and isolating experience. On exiting that relationship the isolation can be magnified as the abused person withdraws from social activities and perhaps becomes cut off from support. This is often the result of the immense shame abused people feel on account of their disempowerment and their maltreatment by the sociopath in their life. Let's take a closer look at the phenomenon of shame.

Shame

In our experience, shame is the greatest barrier for individuals trying to move on. Shame and a growing wariness of others can make it hard for such people to open up about the true extent of their unhappy situation. The situation becomes more desperate if earlier attempts to gain understanding have been met with incredulity. Wariness coupled with deep and toxic shame can render the abused person inactive. Children, for instance, often learn from bitter experience that telling someone else about abuse at home can result in negative, even detrimental, reactions.

Most of the time, shame is a normal and healthy human emotion. A healthy sense of shame keeps our feet on the ground and reminds us of appropriate boundaries. We are human and we make mistakes. Feeling normal levels of shame is giving ourselves permission to be human. A healthy amount of shame can deepen our sense of personal power, helping us to recognize our limits and to redirect our energies to more fruitful pursuits. But too much shame for too long can be harmful and demoralizing. John Bradshaw, author of *Healing the Shame that Binds You*, calls this "toxic shame" and argues that it can become a central part of oneself, leading to profound feelings of isolation.[2] It is an internalized emotion that can lead us to feel defective, beyond remedy.

It is not uncommon for people who experienced the shame and deprivation that goes with having a sociopath in the family to face difficulties in their adult relationships. Individuals who have experienced trauma at the hands of a sociopath in childhood may unwittingly seek out or attract needy and narcissistic types in adulthood. Shame in the children of sociopaths can be intense and hard to shake off, for it originates from the trauma of childhood abandonment.

In her powerful book *The Drama of the Gifted Child,* Alice Miller describes the notion of abandonment trauma.[3] This type of trauma occurs when damage is caused as a result of something *not* happening to an individual—for example, not feeling loved, nurtured, or protected. We can't do justice to Miller's body of work in this space, but we do recommend those interested to read her work (see Resources). In essence, being abandoned by a sociopathic parent who is physically present but emotionally absent can leave a child bewildered to the point of despair. In order to develop as healthy human beings, children need to mirror the actions of an adult caretaker who is both physically and emotionally present. A baby is completely dependent on its parents, whose love and care is essential. Denied his or her basic needs, a child must find ways to avoid being abandoned. Many children in this situation try to reverse the natural order: They take care of their parents, as opposed to the other way around. But this often leads to a paradoxical situation in which the child is nevertheless abandoned.

Many children of sociopathic, neglectful parents try to compensate by becoming caregivers. This can lead to excessive concern with pleasing others and paying disproportionate attention to the care of others, at the expense of a proper focus on oneself. Overwhelmingly, the children or partners of sociopaths tend to put others' needs first. They may feel they deserve the pain and trauma that goes with living with a sociopath; they usually rationalize that, after all, it was they and no one else who got them into this mess. This sort of thinking has a circularity about it, and if not interrupted and eventually terminated may drive a person nearly crazy.

Coping Emotionally

The decision to change a situation of sociopathic abuse can be slow and laborious, or it may be experienced in a "Eureka!" moment. One barrier to seeing the situation for what it is—abuse and trauma—is lack of self-confidence and self-belief, or a fear of "going it alone"; another might be that the relationship is a long-term one with children involved. In that case the timing and nature of the departure from the relationship can matter greatly. All the same, one day the abused person will usually find the courage to break free, or the sociopath will walk out, probably without warning, leaving a whole lot of debris in his wake. Suddenly all alone, the abused person is left to contend with his or her grief and loss.

This phase can be bewildering and frightening. People react differently and take different lengths of time to come to terms with what has happened. Even so, you may be surprised by the strength of your feelings. It is normal to experience a mix of emotions. You may feel:

frightened—that the same thing will happen again, or that you might lose control of your feelings and break down

helpless—that something really bad happened and you could do nothing about it, leaving you feeling vulnerable and overwhelmed

angry—about what has happened and at whoever was responsible

guilty—that you could have done something to prevent it

sad—particularly if you or other people (your children, perhaps) have been affected

ashamed or embarrassed—that you have strong feelings you can't control, especially if you need others to support you

relieved—that the danger is over and that the cause of the danger has gone

hopeful—that your life will return to normal; people often start to feel more positive about things quite soon after a trauma

We liken the process to that of grieving. How we cope depends on our unique temperament and circumstances, but predictable stages of grief tend to ensue.

Stages of Grieving

Following a trauma of any magnitude, many of us experience various stages of grief. We don't necessarily go through the stages one by one, in a neat linear way. There is no typical response to loss; grief is as individual as our lives. Still, the most commonly recognized stages, as defined by Elisabeth Kübler-Ross, are denial, anger, bargaining, depression, and acceptance.[4] Not everyone goes through all of them, or in that order, but knowing about them can equip us to cope better when we do experience them.

◆ ◆ ◆ Denial

According to Kübler-Ross and Kessler, the first stage of grieving is concerned with surviving the loss. In this stage, the world becomes meaningless and overwhelming. Life makes no sense. We are in a state of shock and denial. We go numb. We wonder how we can go on. We find it difficult simply to get through each day. These are survival tactics that help to pace our feelings of grief. It is "nature's way" of letting in only as much as we can handle. As we accept the reality of the loss, we start to ask questions and, unknowingly, begin the healing process. Without being aware of it we become a little stronger day by day, and the denial begins to fade. It is only as we proceed that all the feelings come to the surface, by which time we should be better equipped to handle them.

◆ ◆ ◆ Anger

Anger is a necessary stage of the healing process. Be willing and unafraid to feel your anger, even though it may seem endless. The more you truly feel it, the more it will begin to dissipate and the more you will heal. There are many other emotions beneath the anger, and you will get to them in time, but anger is the emotion we are most used to managing. The truth is that anger often feels like it has no bounds. It can extend not only to the sociopath who has left your life but also to your friends and your family, and to yourself.

Beneath anger is often pain. It is natural to feel pain at being deserted and abandoned, but we live in a society that fears anger. You may get angry at others now that you are no longer with the sociopath. Your anger is a driving force, something that has the propensity to propel you forward, and in that sense it is your ally, your friend. A connection made from the strength of anger feels better than nothing, so sometimes it is something we hold on to. We usually know more about suppressing anger than about feeling it. The anger is just another indication of the intensity of your grief and sense of loss.

◆ ◆ ◆ Bargaining

After a loss, bargaining may provide a temporary respite. Kübler-Ross and Kessler observe that in this phase, the grieving person's conversations become full of "If only" or "What if" statements—such as, "What if I wake up and realize this has all been a bad dream?" We want life to be returned to what it was; we want it restored. The "if onlys" cause us to find fault in ourselves and what we think we could have done differently. We are often willing to do anything to avoid feeling the pain of a loss. In this state we may drink too much alcohol, take prescribed medication or illicit drugs, or eat too much to dampen or dull our senses and block the pain. But doing so means we remain in the past, trying to circumvent the hurt.

◆ ◆ ◆ Depression

After bargaining, our attention switches from the past to the here and now. Empty feelings may present themselves, and we may experience grief on a deeper level. We withdraw from life and feel intense sadness. This stage seems as though it will last forever. It is important to understand that this depression or period of low mood is not a sign of mental illness but is rather an appropriate response to loss.

Depression after a loss is too often seen as unnatural: a state to be fixed, something to snap out of. The first question to ask yourself is whether or not the situation you are in is actually depressing and, if so, whether depression is a normal and appropriate response. Not to experience some level of depression would be unusual after a marriage or family breakdown or an extreme emotional assault. Once you are fully able to take in the nature of the loss, the realization of what you have experienced is understandably depressing. We may need to accept that if grief is a process of healing, then depression is one of the many necessary steps along the way.

◆ ◆ ◆ Acceptance

Acceptance is often confused with the notion of being "all right" with a given situation, or of forgiving others (in our case the sociopath and/or his apathetic followers) for what has happened. This is not what we mean when we use the term "acceptance" here. Most people never reach a point of feeling all right about the losses and traumas they have experienced. What this stage is about is accepting the reality of the situation and recognizing that this new reality is permanent; in other words, arriving at a point where we learn to live with it, and where living with it becomes the new norm. In resisting the new norm, people cling to the hope of maintaining life as it was before. In time, however, we come to see that we can't maintain the past in the present. It has been changed and we must adjust. Hence we learn to accept new roles for ourselves and for others.

Finding acceptance may simply entail having more good days than bad ones. We can't replace our old lives and relationships, but we can make new connections and meaningful new relationships. Instead of denying our feelings, we must listen to our needs in order to move, change, grow, and evolve. Once grief has been given its rightful stint, this is a time to live again.

Managing Anxiety, Stress, and Anger in the Early Days

Anxiety, stress, and anger may result from continued association with a sociopath, or from the process of grieving for the relationship you thought you had with the sociopath before you discovered it was phony. Left unchecked, anxiety and stress can build up and lead to anxiety disorders. When we become stressed or angry, our body's levels of fight-or-flight hormones such as cortisol and adrenaline increase. If we don't then either run or fight, these stress hormones stay in the body, affecting our immune system, sleep, and emotional well-being. Stress hormones have been linked with both heart disease and depression. We estimate that a sizeable number of referrals to psychiatric services for anxiety disorders and depression arise from circumstances involving sociopathic abuse. To prevent this from occurring to you, it is important to deal with anxiety and find ways to manage it.

If you find you have a particular problem with stress and anger, this section of the book may help you. Here we'll examine some techniques that may help you manage stress and anger in the early days after suffering a trauma.[5]

♦ ♦ ♦ Pressing the Pause Button

The first step is to press the pause button, so to speak, and buy some time out from your anger and frustration. You might want to ask yourself the following questions:

What will I do to press the pause button?
You might try walking away, counting to ten, distracting yourself, keeping quiet, or just biting your tongue.

What things might I try to stop me from getting angry?
Possibilities include breathing, self-talk, exercise, talking to someone you trust, and practicing assertiveness.

One way to look at situations in which you easily get angry is by mentally dividing your thoughts into hot and cool ones, and then deliberately choosing to focus more on the cool ones, to the extent possible. For example:

Hot thoughts	Cool thoughts
How dare he!	Don't let it wind you up.
She's trying to humiliate me.	I may not have all the facts.
It's the same thing over again.	It might be different this time.

It can be difficult to identify your thoughts, so another way of looking at the issue is to view thoughts as "self-talk," or talking things over in your head. This is a normal thing to do and it can be really helpful. You can use self-talk to help when you are going into a difficult situation in which you may possibly get angry. You can also use it to get through a difficult situation, or afterward to review what you did.

♦♦♦ Tackling Stress

There are hundreds, if not thousands, of books on dealing with stress or anxiety, but to keep things simple, here are our top-ten tips for tackling stress, adapted from those of the U.K. mental health charity MIND:[6]

1. *Make the connection.* Could the fact that you're feeling "not right" be a response to what the sociopath has put you through?

2. *Take regular breaks.* Give yourself a brief break whenever you feel things are getting on top of you.

3. *Learn to relax.* Follow a simple routine to relax your muscles and slow your breathing (example below).

4. *Get better organized.* Make a list of the problems you need to tackle and deal with one task at a time.

5. *Sort out your worries.* Divide them into those that you can do something about (either now or soon) and those that you can't. There's no point in worrying about things you can't change.

6. *Change what you can.* Look at the problems that can be resolved, and get whatever help is necessary to sort them out. Learn to say "no."

7. *Look at your long-term priorities.* What can you off-load, or change? How can you get your life into better balance?

8. *Improve your lifestyle.* Find time to eat properly, get plenty of exercise, and get enough sleep. Avoid drinking and smoking too much. However much you believe these habits can help you to relax, they tend to have the opposite effect.

9. *Confide in someone.* Don't keep your emotions bottled up.

10. *Focus on the positive aspects of your life.*

◆ ◆ ◆ Learning to Relax

Here is a set of simple instructions to help you relax:

1. Close your eyes, and breathe slowly and deeply.

2. Locate any areas of bodily tension, and try to relax the muscles involved; imagine the tension disappearing.

3. Relax each part of your body, in turn, from your feet to the top of your head.

4. As you focus on each part of your body, think of warmth, heaviness, and relaxation.

5. After twenty minutes, take some deep breaths and stretch your body.

◆ ◆ ◆ Managing Frustration

People with anger difficulties often talk about first becoming frustrated, and then getting angry after the frustration sets in. Frustration is an emotion that we all experience from time to time. It develops when you are thwarted or hindered while trying to do something or reach a goal. It is the feeling you get when you expect a different outcome from what really happens. Although frustration can be helpful, as it can lead to new ways of thinking about a problem, it is basically about not getting what we want, or about getting what we *don't* want. Finding ways to manage frustration may improve our sense of well-being in everyday life.

There are a variety of factors that can trigger frustration. These include:

thoughts—unrealistic expectations, plans, or ideas for yourself or others (such thoughts may include the words "should," "must," or "ought," e.g., "She *should* do what I told her")

situations—particular places or tasks you would rather avoid

relationships—contact with people whom you would prefer not to see

Frustration often occurs when we have expectations for ourselves or others that are too high or that are simply unattainable. In such cases we may have to alter our perspective or way of thinking. We may need to become what is called in the world of therapeutics "frustration tolerant." To be frustration tolerant is to continue living a balanced, healthy life despite encountering repeated interferences and obstacles. How frustration tolerant we are refers to how robust we are in the face of life's stressors and challenges. If someone gets easily frustrated when she cannot get what she wants, she is said to have low frustration tolerance. Her frustration is intolerable and she can't cope. This way of thinking leads to an increased discomfort. People with low frustration tolerance underestimate their ability to cope with discomfort; they might say, "I can't bear it!" or, "I can't stand it!" The words we use to describe such situations matter. Describing something as "intolerable" can make it appear more daunting or off-putting than it actually is.

We can stand frustrating times if we choose to think about them in a different way. The best approach might be to find ways of controlling the degree of frustration we experience in daily life. This may be achieved by changing the things we do or the thoughts we have when we feel frustrated. Alternatively, if there is nothing we can do to change a situation, it may consume less energy if we are able to learn to accept and tolerate the uncomfortable experiences.

The most effective approach to overcoming low frustration is to develop an attitude of high frustration tolerance. This is the ability to tolerate discomfort while waiting to get what you want. Basically it is about toughing things out. Increasing our tolerance for frustration helps us to experience normal levels of healthy annoyance in response to being blocked. High frustration tolerance enables people to be more effective at solving problems or accepting things that, at least at present, cannot be changed.

Examples of high-frustration-tolerance statements are:

- This is an uncomfortable situation, but I can stand the discomfort.

- This situation is hard to bear, but I can bear it—some difficult things are worth tolerating.

- Even if I feel like I can't take it anymore, past experience has shown that I probably can.

To increase your frustration tolerance, ask these types of questions:

- Can I remember being in this situation before and coping with it?

- Is it true that I can't stand this situation, or is it just that I don't like the situation?

- Is this situation truly unbearable, or is it really just very difficult to bear?

Being less extreme in our judgment of negative situations can help us have less extreme emotional responses, such as energy-depleting anger. Many situations are difficult to tolerate, but we need to remember at such times that we have tolerated similar situations in the past.

It is important to understand that we aren't saying that every negative situation should be endured. We are talking here about developing tolerance for everyday frustrations, not for abuse. Indeed, some empathic people may have a greater tendency to talk themselves out of being upset by a sociopath's mistreatment of them: "Oh, it's not so bad that he says unkind things to me. At least he doesn't beat me." Learn to distinguish between a healthy level of tolerance for life's ordinary frustrations and a willingness to put up with sociopathic abuse.

◆ ◆ ◆ Expressing Anger in a Healthy Way

Venting means releasing pent-up feelings of anger or getting things off your chest. Venting is often explosive and can be an act of aggression. When people vent their anger to the person they're angry with, they often feel better immediately afterward. However, not long after that, most people report feeling guilty, ashamed, or sad for the hurt they caused another person. Originally, venting was thought to be helpful and healthy for reducing anger difficulties.

However, recent evidence suggests that venting is not healthy because it increases the chances of further anger in the future.

The following steps may help you express your anger in a healthier way:

1. Recognize and label your angry feelings: "I am feeling angry because…"

2. Is the incident that has made you angry important or unimportant?

3. If it is important, can you influence or control it?

4. If it is important and you can influence or control it, are there strategies you can use to implement the actions? If so, list them. If it is not important, dismiss it and move on.

♦ ♦ ♦ Catching Yourself Dwelling on the Negative

Rumination involves dwelling on or thinking deeply about something. Everybody does it from time to time, but some forms of rumination can be unhealthy. People ruminate by bringing thoughts, memories, and imagined events to mind and going over and over them. If what you're ruminating about is an unpleasant topic, then doing so can have a negative impact on your mental health. Ruminating about the darker side of life can lead to anxiety, depression, and anger. Rumination can impair thinking, motivation, concentration, memory, and problem solving, and can drive away people who might be willing to support us. It can also increase stress.

There are several types of negative rumination:

Anxious rumination involves dwelling on thoughts about bad things that might happen to us or to others. People with social anxiety go over what others might think of them, and over things they think they've done wrong in a certain situation. People with health anxiety dwell on worries that they might contract, or already have, a serious illness.

Depressive rumination involves dwelling on the causes and consequences of feeling depressed (lack of motivation or hopelessness). Depression can be related to a fear of anger, and ruminating can arise from a fear of hurting others.

Angry rumination may focus on injustice, angry memories, thoughts of revenge, or angry afterthoughts. The way we think about things affects our emotions and our bodies. If, for example, you are hungry and you see your favorite meal, your mouth will water. Even just thinking about or imagining your favorite meal will have a similar effect, because our thoughts stimulate areas of the brain responsible for digestion. Likewise, ruminating about an unpleasant interaction, for example, will trigger the fight-or-flight response and get our bodies revved up.

What happens when you ruminate or dwell on negative events? It helps to think about the physical, behavioral, and emotional effects of rumination. What do you ruminate about? What are the usual triggers? What are the consequences? As with all aspects of anger, the first task is to recognize *when* you are doing it. So whenever you start to dwell on something that makes you feel angry, remind yourself that you are ruminating—"WARNING! I'm ruminating"—and stop as quickly as possible. If ruminating has become a habit, however, this may be easier said than done. And as with all habits, patience and practice of new behaviors are essential. Here is a plan of action:

1. When you find yourself dwelling on what has happened, say to yourself, "Stop ruminating!"

2. Calm yourself with breathing, relaxation, meditation, or exercise (see the tips for relaxation, above).

3. Question the purpose and value of ruminating. Ask yourself:

   ◆ Would I advise a friend to think in this way?

   ◆ What would a friend say to me if she knew I was ruminating?

   ◆ Am I looking at the whole picture?

   ◆ Does it really matter that much?

   ◆ What would I say about this in five years' time? Will it be that important?

   ◆ Do I apply one set of rules or standards to myself and another to other people?

   ◆ Have I got the facts right?

   ◆ Am I just tired and irritable?

4. Challenge your perspective of the situation:

   ◆ Maybe there's been a mistake or I've misunderstood.

   ◆ Have I checked that there's no other reason for this situation?

- Have I explained myself clearly?
- What's this doing to my health?
- Have I jumped to conclusions too quickly?
- Ruminating like this may be harming me.
- I will act when I'm calm and have thought about it clearly.

5. Learn and practice mindfulness techniques. When people ruminate they tend to either revisit past injustices or go into the future and fantasize about revenge or worrisome scenarios. So bringing your mind into the present moment can be a powerful strategy. Say to yourself, "Be here now." Another mindfulness technique is to focus your mind on your senses and become aware of what is around you: the sights, sounds, smells, and textures.

6. Set aside rumination time. This is a useful technique to follow if you find you can't stop ruminating.

   a. Set aside a regular time each day for ruminating. Allow no more than about fifteen to twenty minutes once a day; set an alarm clock. Pick a time when you are free of interruptions.

   b. Select a place to ruminate, somewhere you don't associate with relaxation (i.e., not your bed or favorite chair). Some people sit at the foot of the stairs or at a table in an upright chair. This will be the only place you should ruminate.

   c. On a piece of paper write down your negative thoughts, all the things you are dwelling on.

   d. Stop when time's up; remember, set an alarm clock.

   e. If any negative thoughts come up during the day, write them down on a piece of paper, and tell yourself to stop thinking about them until your allotted time.

You will begin to understand your anger if you accept that your emotions and feelings are neither good nor bad but are actually messengers. Then you can ask yourself what they are trying to tell you. When you feel anger or emotions related to anger (upset, annoyance, frustration, resentment, feeling judgmental), ask yourself: Is my anger masking feelings of fear or loss?

If so, then acknowledge those feelings. If not, ask yourself if your ideas and beliefs are being violated. Try to revise those ideas by changing them to more flexible ones.

When the Stress
and Anxiety Don't Shift

After exiting a traumatic relationship with a sociopath, and with sufficient support from friends and family, you might hope that it's possible to move straightforwardly through the stages of coming to terms with the situation, from initial trauma to acceptance. However, no one can predict the outcome of this recovery process. Even with the best intentions, some people end up enduring persistent stress and anxiety—an experience similar to, if not the same as, post-traumatic stress disorder. (Because it has primarily been identified by observing survivors of a specific range of traumatic events, such as combat and disaster, the term "PTSD" fails to capture the consequences of prolonged, repeated trauma such as instances when a person is under the control of an abuser and is unable to flee, as may be the case in families where abuse is taking place.)

PTSD is a severe anxiety disorder that can develop after exposure to any event that results in psychological trauma. According to Judith Herman, an expert on surviving trauma, captivity that brings the targeted person into prolonged contact with the perpetrator of the abuse creates a special type of relationship. She defines it as one of coercive control. This is equally true when the individual is rendered captive by physical, economic, social, or psychological means, as in the cases of battered partners or spouses and abused children.[7]

PTSD arises due to deregulation of the fear system. Fear is a necessary emotion at times of danger, and like anger is followed by a stress response— fighting, freezing, or fleeing. This survival system depends on our ability to appraise threats in order to initiate survival behavior. Once the threat or trauma is over, the fear system normally calms down after a few days or weeks. In PTSD this system fails to reset to normal, keeping the sufferer hyperalert, on the lookout in case the event happens again.[8] Hence, PTSD is more enduring than the more commonly seen fight-or-flight response (also known as acute stress response). The trauma inflicted on an individual threatens her psychological integrity and overwhelms her ability to cope.

The disorder is characterized by involuntary, persistent remembering or reliving of the traumatic event or events in flashbacks, vivid memories, and recurrent dreams. Usually this is accompanied by problems such as depression, substance abuse, and anxiety disorders. The person may feel emotionally numb—for example, feeling detached from others. Other symptoms include sleep problems, difficulty in concentrating, and being emotionally labile (moods go up and down: the person is elated one moment, miserable the next). Chronically traumatized people are often hypervigilant and agitated. Over time they may also complain of numerous physical symptoms; tension headaches, gastrointestinal disturbances, and abdominal, back, or pelvic pain are extremely common. Affected individuals also frequently complain of tremors, choking sensations, or nausea. Repeated trauma appears to intensify the physiological symptoms.

For a formal diagnosis of PTSD to be made, the symptoms should have lasted more than one month and be causing significant impairment in the person's social, occupational, or other important areas of functioning. When the symptoms are mild and have been present for less than four weeks after the traumatic events last occurred, the guidelines recommend keeping a watchful eye and waiting. But determining how to manage the chaos, material losses, grief, and anger is based on the individual person, and how and when he or she regains control.

The clinical literature points to an association between bodily disorders and childhood trauma. Some survivors of prolonged childhood abuse develop severe dissociation, cutting themselves off and becoming detached from their feelings and other people. At the other extreme, one study conducted in 1989 described a process the researchers called "mind-fragmenting operations," where abused children were deluded into thinking that their abusive parents were good parents."[9]

Prolonged trauma at the hands of a sociopath may have emotional impacts, such as protracted depression. Here the chronic symptoms of PTSD combine with the symptoms of depression, producing what has been called the "survivor triad" of insomnia, nightmares, and psychosomatic complaints. The humiliated rage of the traumatized person adds to the burden. He has been unable to express anger at his perpetrator; to do so would have jeopardized his survival. So even when released from the perpetrator's grip, he continues to be afraid of expressing his anger. Furthermore, the individual often carries a burden of unexpressed anger against all those who remained indifferent and failed to help. Efforts to control this rage may exacerbate his social withdrawal and paralysis of initiative, while occasional outbursts of rage against others may further alienate him and prevent the restoration of relationships. Internalization of rage may result in self-hatred, even thoughts of suicide. Even though major depression is frequently diagnosed in survivors of prolonged abuse, the connection with the preceding trauma is frequently lost. Hence patients are incompletely treated because the traumatic origins of the intractable depression have not been recognized.

Depression, severe anxiety, and fear commonly stem from traumatic memories. People distressed by such memories may constantly relive them through nightmares or flashbacks, and may withdraw from their family or social circle in order to avoid exposing themselves to reminders of those memories. They may become physically aggressive, moody, or argumentative, causing difficulties in relationships with their family, spouse or partner, and children. Sometimes they resort to substance abuse in order to deal with the anxiety. If symptoms of apathy, impulsive behavior, sleeplessness, or irritability persist, the person may want to discuss this with his or her family doctor and seek the help of a psychotherapist.

The management of traumatic memories is important when treating PTSD. Traumatic memories are stressful and can emotionally overwhelm a person's existing coping mechanisms. When simple objects such as a photograph, or events such as a birthday party, evoke traumatic memories, people often try to remove the unwanted memory from their minds in order to proceed with life, but this approach usually has only limited success. Over time the frequency of these triggers or memory joggers diminishes for most people, and for some the number of intrusive memories diminishes rapidly as the person adjusts to the situation. For others, however, they may continue for decades and interfere with the person's mental, physical, and social well-being.

Several psychotherapies have been developed that weaken or prevent the formation of traumatic memories. Cognitive behavioral therapies have been found effective in reducing the emotional distress and negative thought patterns associated with traumatic memories in those with PTSD and depression. One such therapy is trauma-focused therapy. This involves bringing the traumatic memory or memories to mind, and with the aid of a therapist restructuring the way the memories are thought about. Another is eye-movement desensitization and reprocessing (EMDR). This involves elements of both exposure therapy (in which you systematically confront your fears) and cognitive behavioral therapy (which addresses unhelpful ways of thinking about your situation, and the things you do as a result)—although there is still some debate as to whether it works. EMDR begins by identifying disturbing memories, cognitions, and sensations. Then the negative thoughts that are associated with each memory are uncovered. While both memory and thought are held in mind, the person follows a moving object with her eyes. Afterward, a positive thought about the memory is discussed in an effort to replace the negative thought associated with the memory.

Pharmacological methods for erasing traumatic memories are currently being researched, although this raises ethical concerns. The use of drugs to blunt the impact of traumatic memories treats human emotional reactions to life events as a medical issue, which may not necessarily be a good thing and may expose individuals to unnecessary risk. If drug treatments are administered unnecessarily—when, for example, a person could learn to cope without drugs—the person may needlessly be exposed to side effects. And the loss of painful memories may actually end up causing more harm than good. Painful, frightening, or even traumatic memories can serve to teach us to avoid certain situations or experiences. By removing those memories, their function in warning and protecting individuals may be lost.

Existing medications can sometimes be helpful following a trauma, but it is important for the person diagnosed with PTSD to see a medical doctor for regular checkups. There have been significant advances in the medical treatment of PTSD; nevertheless, as is the case with other anxiety disorders, few long-term trials have been performed, and there is a lack of data on the effectiveness of treatment. The American Psychiatric Association's position is that medication can help to control the symptoms of PTSD. The symptom relief that medication provides allows many patients to participate more effectively in psychotherapy when their condition may otherwise prohibit it.

Antidepressant medications may be particularly helpful in treating the core symptoms of PTSD, either alone or in combination with psychotherapy.

As mentioned, individuals with PTSD can also become ill with depression. Depression can be treated either with antidepressant medication or with talking treatments such as counseling or psychotherapy—or through a combination of both medication and talk therapy. It is important in such cases, when the PTSD symptoms persist, to speak about them openly with someone and get professional help.

The important message to take from all this is that by reaching out for support, seeking medical advice and treatment, and developing new coping skills, individuals can at the very least learn to effectively manage the symptoms of PTSD and, better still, to overcome the problem in time.

Establishing Boundaries and Regaining Control of Your Life

ONCE YOU HAVE ENDED the sociopathic relationship, dusted yourself off, and regained some control over your life, there are decisions to be made about the longer term. Sociopaths don't change their behavior. Unfortunately, they leave that responsibility to the rest of us. Sociopaths have no reason to change because the motivation and opportunities persist for them to continue abusing other people. That means you will most likely have to modify your own behavior to guard yourself against further mistreatment. This chapter examines how to do so.

Dealing with an Isolated Encounter

In the case of a one-off brush with a sociopath, chances are all you need to do is establish boundaries within your relationship so you can regain some control over the situation. For instance, if you work with a colleague who has sociopathic tendencies and you fear she will attempt to sabotage your work or damage your reputation in some way, keep a record of her correspondence, including e-mails. Another way to reassert control is to restrict future communications. For instance, you could insist that all correspondence go through a third party; if the option is available, you might even avoid communicating with your abusive colleague altogether. It depends on your work circumstances and the circumstances within which the sociopath operates. If the sociopath has some jurisdiction over you—as your boss or supervisor, for example—you may need to consider making a formal complaint of harassment.

Addressing Bullying and Harassment

Bullying and harassment in the workplace should not be tolerated. Harassment is unwanted conduct that has the purpose or effect of violating an individual's dignity or creating an intimidating, hostile, degrading, humiliating, or offensive environment for that individual. Sexual harassment in particular is is one of the most common forms of harassment. Bullying is characterized as offensive, intimidating, malicious, or insulting behavior, or an abuse or misuse of power through means that undermine, humiliate, denigrate, or injure the recipient. In the U.S., harassment is considered a form of employment discrimination that violates Title VII of the Civil Rights Act of 1964, as well as other laws. The Equal Employment Opportunity Commission is the federal agency responsible for enforcing employment law and for investigating charges of employment discrimination, including harassment. See Resources for the EEOC's contact information.[1]

It is good practice for employers to provide examples of what is unacceptable behavior in their company. These may include the following:

+ spreading malicious rumors or insulting someone (particularly on the grounds of age, race, sex, disability, sexual orientation, or religious belief)

+ copying memos that are critical about someone to others who don't need to know

+ ridiculing or demeaning someone—picking on them or setting them up to fail

+ exclusion from a team or a task

+ victimization

+ unfair treatment, such as being asked to do unnecessary tasks, or penalizing without cause

+ overbearing supervision, or other misuse of power or position

+ unwelcome sexual advances—touching, standing too close, display of offensive materials, asking for sexual favors, making decisions on the basis of sexual advances being accepted or rejected

◆ making threats or comments about job security without foundation

◆ deliberately undermining a competent worker by overloading and constant criticism

◆ preventing an individual's progress by intentionally blocking promotion or training opportunities

If the bullying occurs at school, as was the case with James (Chapter 1), it is important as a parent or caregiver to communicate your concerns to the school at the earliest opportunity, and to work with the school to resolve the problem. Bullying is often exacerbated by the fact that some of the victim's peers don't want to lose status by associating with him, or are eager to avoid the risk of being bullied themselves, thus increasing the isolation of the person on the receiving end. Bullying is by nature an insidious problem, so if your child's behavior suddenly changes, don't assume it is merely related to hormones and puberty. Instead, talk to her; it could be indicative of something far more troubling. At the time of this book's publication, forty-nine states in the United States have antibullying laws in place for schools.[2]

If the sociopathic bully is a friend or neighbor, be vigilant and record any unusual goings-on. If you are experiencing harassment or intimidating behavior yourself, don't ignore it; most of the time it is unlikely to go away without some kind of action. Don't think it is your fault, and don't fear being labeled a troublemaker for bringing it to the attention of other people and the relevant authorities. People who are involved in harassing behavior often display it as a form of control and "superiority"; if you ignore it, this may be seen by the sociopath as a sign of his or her success.

Even if you have only been harassed once, don't hesitate to contact someone for help. If the situation warrants it—for instance, if your safety or someone else's is at risk, or if property has been damaged—inform your local police and ask them for help. Another option is to seek legal help from an attorney. At work, you could talk to someone in human resources or, if your company offers such a service, to an employee resource counselor. You could even seek the help of a professional therapist. If you are in any way worried that there may be actual physical danger or that violence may be threatened, do not confront the person who is harassing you. Instead, call the police at once. If you decide to approach the person responsible for harassing you, take care for your safety. Do *not* go alone; take a friend or relative with you. Taking a witness will allow you to have a third-party account of what was said and done; the person harassing you cannot then claim that you didn't ask him to stop. Above all, your safety is paramount; do not place yourself in unnecessary danger.

Is It Ever Advisable to Tell Someone They Are Sociopathic?

We don't advise you to confront someone with the notion that they are sociopathic, narcissistic, or psychopathic—or for that matter borderline—even if you are absolutely certain they exhibit the traits. Even if they occasionally appear to be aware that they don't react to situations like other people, sociopaths rarely think badly of themselves. Being relatively unemotional, they can be fearless. Often they use this to their advantage by staying calm when others are afraid. Trying to make a sociopath feel remorse, guilt, or shame is useless and can encourage them to fake their feelings in an attempt to "go along" with the game.

Whether someone knows or is informed that they are sociopathic depends a lot on their social and cultural background. Nowadays, with the omnipresence of the Internet and social media, it must be hard for sociopaths not to know something of the phenomenon of sociopathy or personality disorders. And their self-absorbed nature makes it likely that many of them have read widely on the issue and even diagnosed themselves.

Recovery from Prolonged Contact with a Sociopath

Full recovery from a longer-term traumatic encounter with a sociopath means recapturing your zeal for life. This requires a certain amount of self-growth. Getting over the experience is not always easy. It can be a battle, difficult and discouraging at times. The good news is that the vast majority of us get there in the end—but recovering from the experience often requires us to challenge the perspectives and rules that have sustained our belief systems and the belief systems of those around us. This can cause conflict before bringing us relief or resolution, because often the way we live our life is something handed down to us from our parents and shaped by the culture we're immersed in.

A growing body of literature suggests that recovery is characterized by predictable stages and milestones (see Figure 2). Within each stage there are developmental tasks and skills to master, perspectives to develop, and issues to address before moving to the next stage. Change not only comes about in recognizable stages, but it is also more likely to happen when changing is important to us, and when we are confident in pulling it off. If this makes it sound easy, we acknowledge that it isn't. For most of us, change doesn't occur in a neat and linear fashion; in fact, the direction of travel can be a little bit messy, with movement back and forth. Things begin to steady as you gain confidence in the process. Thankfully, most people get there eventually.

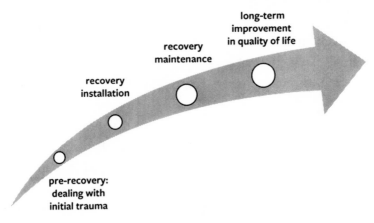

FIGURE 2. The recovery process

Change requires us to actively engage in the process. We have assets, both internal and external—collectively called recovery capital—that support us in dealing with changing circumstances. Every one of us possesses internal reserves of recovery capital that initiate and sustain our recovery, but sometimes we need a little help in identifying what we've got. Sometimes to aid the process we also need a change in self-perception, or to "repair" our identity.

It can help to seek out others who have a shared goal. People recovering from a traumatic relationship with a sociopath often find recovery-supportive friendships beneficial. Such friendships need to be natural (reciprocal), accessible to you at times of greatest need, and potentially enduring. It can also make a real difference if a positive person is around to witness your change. In her book *Banished Knowledge: Facing Childhood Injuries,* author and child-abuse expert Alice Miller identifies this sort of person as an "enlightened witness," someone willing to support a harmed individual and to help him gain understanding of his past experiences.[3]

In this context an enlightened witness is anyone who is insightful and empathetic enough to help you face up to your difficulties and regain your autonomy. If you are isolated and no such witness is immediately available, social media and the Internet can prove a helpful route to finding support. The change process is often messy, so if you become engaged in peer support you may find yourself flitting between roles, from acting helpless to engaging in the act of helping others. This is entirely normal and healthy given the tentative nature of the recovery process.

Practical Steps

There are certain guidelines that are almost universal in preventing further mistreatment at the hands of a sociopath. They are outlined here. Some of these may involve learning new skills and adopting new behaviors that govern how you relate to others.

✦ ✦ ✦ Establishing Personal Boundaries

It is important to reestablish your personal boundaries. One of the best moves you can make is to introduce and reinforce new rules of engagement with the sociopath. This may or may not include a rule of "no contact." A rule of no contact is easier said than implemented, but it can be very necessary in order to prevent further trauma. The move is a lot easier to carry off if at the final showdown the sociopath walks out of your life; nevertheless, *you* may have to initiate the rule and take affirmative action yourself. The right approach—whether merely to limit contact or to apply a no-contact rule— depends on your individual circumstances, but whatever route you take, stay alert to the sociopath's persistent games and stand firm; sociopaths have a tendency to draw you in again and again.

✦✦✦ Limiting Contact

Many people involved with a sociopath limit contact at the point when the drama reaches a critical pitch. Each person's situation is unique, however, and it is best to determine for yourself what amount of contact you are prepared to accept. For a parent whose partner or ex-partner is a sociopath, this is an especially difficult, stressful, and confusing time. Not only are you dealing with the trauma of a destructive relationship; you are also working out how to handle future relations in order to protect your children.

It is not uncommon for a sociopath to behave badly and in an extreme fashion as soon as he realizes you want to reduce or stop contact. He may become disruptive and manipulative in an attempt to regain control. On the plus side, most sociopaths eventually give up hassling and manipulating you—usually when they set their sights on a new target. Nevertheless, limiting contact with a sociopath requires you to be firm. You have to learn to assert yourself and your needs, which will help you in your own recovery.

That said, if you think the sociopath is potentially dangerous, and you perceive that you, another adult, or any children are still at risk, you should seek help from the authorities: the police, social services, and/or legal advisers. Another important piece of advice is to maintain written records of all agreements and discussions involving adults who may be at risk of harm, and regarding the welfare of children. Keep all written statements in a safe place; you will need ample evidence if you decide to take legal action at a later date.

✦✦✦ Banning Contact

In most circumstances it is probably best to have no contact at all with a person you identify as a sociopath. While it can be quite straightforward to cut ties with someone who is relatively new in your life, if the sociopath is part of your social group or family—for example, a friend or partner of long standing—it becomes more complicated. You should ensure that other friends and acquaintances know you are no longer in contact with the individual concerned, and ask them not to play "go-between." You will also need to make it clear that you don't want to discuss anything about the sociopathic person (or people). Refuse to accept information from a third party. If that person insists, tell them not to involve themselves in this way as it could damage relations between you.

The leaking of communication to and from third parties is the most common mistake people make following the establishment of a no-contact rule. Although you may be naturally curious to hear the third party out, it can reopen wounds to learn what the sociopath is saying about you or doing in her life, so stop people immediately if they begin telling you anything, and let them know you are not prepared to hear or say anything about the person who has abused you. If the third party refuses to respect your wishes, you should consider limiting contact with him or her as well.

For those whose lives have been heavily enmeshed with one or more sociopaths, for instance in a family, a no-contact rule can be extremely hard to apply. You will have to decide whom to cut out completely, as well as what to do about communication with family members who are on the periphery of the situation. Again, you may have to spell out the boundaries to avoid further conflict.

Cutting ties is a painful and terminal action but typically a necessary one. On the upside, it is a significant step on the road to recovery. One way of doing it is to write a frank letter stating that the relationship is over and you don't wish to be contacted again. A phone call or e-mail seems easy, but it can lead to the mistake of getting into continued dialogue and bartering. Once a no-contact rule is set, you will need to make other decisions. Do you remove phone messages without listening to them? Block the person on Facebook and Twitter? Do you accept apologies? Gifts?

If messages are left on an answering machine, or you receive e-mails or calls from the person concerned, you must resist the temptation to respond. If the person catches you unaware and you pick up a call, hang up immediately. Call blocking is another option, and is inexpensive. Sociopaths like playing games with your emotions, and their having access to you after a relationship is over allows the game to continue. If your sociopath does harass you in this way, keep all his communications in case you decide to pursue a harassment charge at some later stage, as this is potential evidence. If you wish to save the evidence but think you would be too tempted to read it or to act on the contents, immediately give any communiqués to a trusted third party or to a lawyer who can store them safely. It is probably advisable to block the sociopath from your e-mail or to change your e-mail address. If anything gets through, delete it as soon as you recognize the sender without opening or reading it (the exception to the rule being if you feel you need it as evidence). Do not get into games with the sociopath by reentering into dialogue.

♦ ♦ ♦ Preventing Lapses in Judgment

Having an enlightened witness around will help to keep the person in recovery (you) on the right path. It is not uncommon to feel isolated in the early days once you are removed from immediate danger, especially if you are in completely new surroundings. After the initial relief has worn off, you may feel disorientated, ambivalent, and lonely. Feeling alone is quite a normal response to change and unfamiliar circumstances, and it's one the sociopath will play on, angered by your snub and the change you have made in the rules of engagement. Often at this point a sociopath will accelerate his games. He may make you question your sanity, your perception of what happened, or everything and everyone you hold dear. He may even feign remorse to try to win you back, a response that is hard to ignore if you are feeling lonely and excluded.

Meanwhile, others who don't know the full extent of your situation may make judgments and disparaging remarks, particularly if you have left a marriage, job, or family. This sort of reaction sadly comes with the territory, as those who make a stand are often harshly judged by others who are uninformed and who look on with untrained eyes. And let us not forget that most of those who criticize you likely belong to the 60 percent of apaths, many of whom may fear your newfound voice and strength. If this happens, just remember it is most likely your freedom of spirit and nonconformity that trigger others' anxiety, rather than anything being discernibly wrong with you. This is why it is important not to withdraw and become isolated at such a critical moment. Instead, the best route out of the situation is to keep good people (including those enlightened witnesses) around you and let them buoy you up until you are confident in your unconventionality and accept it as one of your strengths.

For all your good intentions about maintaining limited contact, or breaking it altogether, you may find that you trip up. There will be situations to look out for and avoid until new behaviors and habits are embedded and become the norm. In the intervening period you need to learn how to keep from setting yourself up and becoming entangled again in the sociopath's life. In some ways, weaning a person off a destructive relationship is like weaning them from an addictive substance or behavior. In both situations the relationship and patterns of behavior are often deeply entrenched. It takes time to gain confidence in one's ability to make what may be sweeping life changes, and time to adopt new sets of behavior. It takes patience and a willingness to learn from trial and error to sustain changes and fully adapt. But one advantage the nonsociopathic have over the sociopathic is the ability to change. The sociopath is unable to do this; his or her persona is fixed. He or she lacks the insight and ability to learn from his or her mistakes. In addition, the socio-path's behavior is fairly predictable. In essence, sociopaths behave the way they do because they are motivated by a need for stimulus and because they seek out opportunities. Figure 3 sums this up diagrammatically.

FIGURE 3. Motivators for sociopathic behavior

Once you understand this fact, it is up to you to identify ways to block opportunities for the sociopath to snare you again. Using the straightfor-ward approaches outlined in this section, it is possible to identify cues and triggers to avoid relapsing into old ways that will have you interacting with the sociopath. Becoming more aware of our former behaviors helps us gain insight, which in turn helps keep us from getting inadvertently (re)trapped in a cycle of sociopathic abuse.

✦✦✦ Avoiding Seemingly Irrelevant Decisions (SIDs)

A seemingly irrelevant decision, or SID, is a decision or choice that may appear unimportant or insignificant on the surface but actually increases the likelihood that the person making it will be placed in a high-risk situa-tion that can cause a relapse into his or her former behavior. A person may ignore, deny, or explain away the importance of these decisions and choices. The identification of SIDs is an important part of the relapse-prevention treatment first devised by psychologists G. Alan Marlatt and J. R. Gordon and used with people with addictive behaviors.[4] We think it is a useful approach for weaning yourself off old behaviors that result in your succumbing to the sociopath's ploys.

Examples of SIDs include:

- Driving past the sociopath's home on your way home from work
- Idly "googling" the sociopath or checking her Facebook page
- Asking after the sociopath to third parties who are still in contact with her
- Finding some reason to send the sociopath an e-mail
- Texting the sociopath on her birthday or some other special occasion

All these are seemingly innocuous but can put you in the path of danger. Perhaps, as you drive past the sociopath's house, she sees you and waves. That one small act gives her license to call you, hooking you in again. Perhaps checking the sociopath's Facebook page makes you feel sad and you begin reminiscing. Before you know it you have sent her a personal message. Curiosity is not a bad thing; it is natural in many circumstances. It is an emotion related to our inquisitiveness and is connected to learning. But in this situation we need to recognize its disastrous consequences and learn to control the impulse.

◆ ◆ ◆ Recognizing the Rule-Violation Effect (RVE)

The rule-violation effect (RVE) may take over when we break our own rules and boundaries, for example a rule of limited contact or no contact with the sociopath. It refers to the tendency of an individual, having made a personal commitment not to contact the sociopath, to revert to uncontrolled contact following a single lapse. You can liken it to a recovering alcoholic who slips and has one drink, and then, feeling defeated by his momentary relapse, gives up and goes on a weeks-long binge. The RVE comes into play when the person attributes the cause of the initial lapse to factors within himself, such as a lack of willpower or feeling like he misses the sociopath (or rather, the person he *believed* the sociopath to be).

The strategies outlined in this chapter aim to help you learn how to prevent the RVE by making you aware of the more-controllable external or situational factors that may trigger a relapse. Knowing these, you can quickly return to the goal of no contact and avoid losing control of the situation and becoming reentangled with the sociopath.

High-Risk Situations

Specific intervention strategies may help you identify and deal with high-risk situations and manage potential lapses. That's the topic of this section.

◆ ◆ ◆ Moods

You may experience low moods, bad moods, increased anxiety, or irritability when you break off contact with the sociopath. These are temporary feelings and will fade over time. You may overreact to things that normally wouldn't bother you. This is common. Try to find new ways of coping with emotions like anger, upset, annoyance, and stress. The following tips may also help you:

- ◆ Discover new ways of dealing with negative feelings rather than ruminating on the past (review Chapter 4).
- ◆ Remind yourself that the feeling is temporary; it will go away.
- ◆ Congratulate yourself for managing life without the sociopath.
- ◆ Ask others to understand and be patient.
- ◆ Do things that make you feel good.
- ◆ Try to get a good night's sleep, and if having trouble sleeping, seek advice.

If you get good or bad news that affects your mood, dwelling on the past or seeking out the sociopath will not change the news or help the situation. It will only reduce your chances of changing your situation. Have a good cry; tell someone how you are feeling. Take slow, deep breaths over a period of a few minutes to help you relax.

◆ ◆ ◆ Habits and Routines

You may have developed certain habits and routines in your life with the sociopath. It is therefore important to consider changing your routine so you don't experience cues and triggers about him—a situation that could lead you to take SIDs, to lapse, or to end up violating newly established rules.

Besides those listed in Chapter 4, here are more pointers for managing stress:

- Work it off by taking a walk in the fresh air.
- Talk to someone you really trust.
- Learn to accept what you cannot change.
- Don't self-medicate with alcohol, too much caffeine, or tranquilizers.
- Get enough sleep and rest.
- Take time out for activities you really enjoy, or try something fresh such as a new exercise program, creative project, or hobby.
- Do something for someone else.
- Deal with one thing at a time.
- Prioritize your day, and only do the things you have to do.
- Don't be afraid to say no.
- Eat good meals at regular times to stabilize your mood.
- Know when you are tired, and do something about it.
- Be realistic about what you can achieve. Forget perfection.

◆◆◆Triggers

A trigger is something that you associate with a particular person or situation, and to which you are likely to respond. Years of conditioning from a sociopath mean that a particular trigger may set off a reaction in you by a process of association, much as a dog can be conditioned to respond to a ringing bell in the same way as it does to food. Here we introduce and adapt some ideas of psychologist B. J. Fogg, who refers to triggers as either "hot" or "cold." A "hot trigger" is something that affects you immediately: someone yelling at you or demanding something of you, or being stuck in a traffic jam. A "cold trigger" is something that affects you indirectly: seeing an actor who looks like the sociopath on television, or receiving a letter with familiar-looking handwriting. A hot trigger forces an immediate response, while the effects of a cold trigger build up over time.[5] Triggers work as a call to action and can cause us to act on impulse. To avoid lapsing into previous behavior it helps to find a way to disconnect our feelings from the object of association. The steps to breaking the connections involve:

Looking for patterns: First, we need to see clearly the things that make us think about the sociopath and other people we have removed from our lives or have lost as a result of changing our behavior. Once we recognize the kinds of things that work as hot or cold triggers—situations that prompt an unhelpful reaction in us—it is useful to a make a mental note of them.

Becoming more "trigger-savvy": Give yourself a chance to analyze your triggers, and see if you can devise ways to break the associations. Maybe just being cognizant of the fact that a trigger can arouse unwanted feelings and memories is enough. Or maybe you need to talk yourself out of reacting whenever a trigger appears uninvited. Understanding how best to dampen the effects of emerging triggers is necessary in driving behavior change. Jill's story is a good example of how to do this:

Jill
. . . .

Jill had not been in contact with her sociopathic father for several months when a message from him appeared in her e-mail inbox. She immediately recognized it as a trigger, and knew that if she even opened the e-mail she would be in a high-risk situation, in jeopardy of responding to him and thus relapsing. Because she was mindful of this possibility she understood the position she was in. Instead of responding to the e-mail on impulse, as she previously might have done, she calmly deleted the message and got back to her other tasks, thus sidestepping the high-risk situation.

How Others Have Coped: Case Histories

Let's hear, in their own words, how some survivors of sociopathic abuse have managed to deal with the resulting trauma.

Nancy Ellen
. . . .

Years of counseling gave me the tools to learn to set boundaries with my narcissistic mother and my sociopathic adult son (my father is deceased, and I am an only child). I have been fortunate to have found quality counselors who utilized the EMDR method. I owe my life to my two wonderful counselors. They helped me to deal with my rage and disappointment and to develop the courage to move forward with my life. I learned to grieve for the loss of my dream to have a loving mother and a loving son. I stopped engaging in any communication with both of them.

I learned to accept what I cannot change, but that does not mean I like it; I will always have post-traumatic stress disorder. The depth of the loss and betrayal of the two people who should be the closest to me has been heart wrenching. There is no getting over the pain, but the anguish diminishes over time. Support groups on the Internet have led me to other survivors—their validation and support is very healing and soothing, and I am able to help others, too.

Colleen

As a child I lived in my head a lot; I escaped into fantasy and daydreams and books. What really saved me was the birth of my first daughter. That awakened in me a powerful instinct to protect and to survive. She was my first true love, the first clean, beautiful, shining soul in a sordid, cynical world. For the first time I was able to feel what was right and what was wrong, and gradually it started dawning on me that I was not the "bad one," but the one who had been wronged. It is still dawning. I'm not there yet.

Paul

My therapy was focused as much on my mother as it was on my marriage. I believed my mother was perfect. Actually, my relationship with her verged on mother worship. She was never wrong; she knew what I needed to do with my life. My school major was her choice, my job was her choice. At times I felt as if my mother were omniscient, weird as that sounds. My dad seemed to have a midlife crisis when I reached puberty. He changed and became a cruel and selfish person and rejected me after that. At twenty-eight I broke the patterns I had with my mother and began making more of my own choices. My entire family came down against it. I stayed away from Mom and began to grow a little.

My earlier counseling was focused on recognizing my emotions. I had learned as a child to ignore them. All emotions were against my mother's religion: love = lust = bad. Anger = rebellion = bad. As my therapy progressed I healed and my emotions thawed out. When my ex-wife cheated on me I got depressed and told her. She denied that I was depressed. "No you are not," she would say, but I knew I was as I had begun to contemplate suicide. But then I realized that suicide was a permanent solution to a temporary problem. I remembered my earlier therapy and let myself feel, and I began to get angry.

My ex-wife was a serial cheater. There were many times when she behaved strangely and I justified it to myself. After the divorce I began remembering these episodes, and a new understanding emerged. Finally I was able to see her as a flawed human, like myself. This didn't mean I contacted her or told her about my insights, because she is on her own journey and probably wouldn't understand. What little contact I have with her has convinced me she is still a narcissist and would take my overtures the wrong way. My current wife is very strong and understands my weaknesses and strengths; we have a serenity that we will not give up for any amount of material comfort or gold.

Lizzie
· · · · · · · · · ·

I was an anxious child, a worrier. As I grew up I came to appreciate that my sister was "different." She could be charming, but she had a cold, callous streak. No one else seemed to notice, and I felt very afraid and alone with my concerns. My mother is also sociopathic, though obviously as a child I had no idea. Most of my mother's unpleasant behavior was directed at people outside the family. At home she was the matriarch whom we all obeyed. I was a little scared of her and feared her rejection. I know I consciously strove to please her, but she was very critical of me.

I finally started to find my own voice in my twenties. It was then that my relations with the family soured. My mother turned very nasty. I think she sensed she was losing control over me. It wasn't until my forties that I began to realize that I couldn't deal with my family anymore—I couldn't take their abuses any longer, so I got away. Leaving the family, stopping contact, was a very traumatizing experience. What has helped me more than anything is having a supportive and loving husband and a wonderful son. I am still wary of other people, and trust is a big issue for me. Coming from a family rife with sociopathy is very stigmatizing. I rarely tell anyone about it. Recently I joined an online group, where I've met others with similar experiences. That has helped relieve me of some of the burden—finally I have somewhere I can offload the guilt and shame. I still feel unnatural for exiting the family in this way. I feel people judge me for it. But it was the right thing to do for my sanity's sake.

Debrieanna

I thought I'd met my Prince Charming and was living in a fairy tale. In reality, I *was* living a fairy tale...his. His reality, what he pretended to be, was a lie. A deceptive mask of his choosing for each person he used, abused, and discarded. The end always justified the means; I was just one of his toys.

Lies, deceit, manipulation. The red flags were there; I chose not to see them. He gaslighted me into believing I was sick, not him. The fairy tale became a nightmare. When he finally left, after planning it for two years, it got worse. He became nasty and cruel. For him, it was a game to win. He couldn't break me, but I lost all trust in everyone, including myself.

How did I get through this? With lots of prayer. Through my faith and trust in God, along with family and friends' emotional support. Good eventually overcame the evil. My life went from my ex's darkness into my Light.

Bryan

I am a confident person now, but I haven't always been. I have had major setbacks in my life, but the way I deal with problems is by talking to those whom I love most. My story is that I had a run-in with my grandmother, the last person you would imagine. She seemed nice on the surface, but used to make odd remarks to me when the two of us were alone. For example, when I was about five years old she said, "Your father doesn't love you or your mom." She made me think my father was going to leave us, when in fact this was far from true; my parents were happy together.

When you are five years old this is upsetting to hear. My grandmother told me these lies on and off for several years. I was so disturbed by them that it affected my behavior. I couldn't sleep at night and felt anxious all the time. Eventually, I told my parents, who were aghast. They weren't angry with me, but they were angry with my grandmother, and rightly so! I have no idea to this day why she picked on me in this way.

We didn't have contact with my grandmother for some time after that, but because my parents thought it wasn't fair for me not to see my grandparents, they eventually agreed to let me see them for a brief visit. I was about nine years old. The visit escalated into one of the most horrific days of my life. My grandmother must have been angry with me for telling my parents about her behavior, and I think she wanted to get back at me. When my grandfather was out of the room she told me awful things about my parents, and other stuff meant for adult ears, disgusting things. She was also very rough with me physically and shoved me around. When I got home I told my parents the visit had gone well, because I was a bit scared and ashamed and doubted it had happened. I doubted myself!

I couldn't hold it in for long. Soon I broke down and told my parents everything. Of course it was hard for me to tell them all the things my grandmother had said, but I felt a lot better afterward. They helped me so much and comforted me. Afterward, I felt like I had made it all up, even though deep down I knew I hadn't. But it was all so absurd. Telling others of my ordeal reassured me and brought me to my senses.

This major setback was something I wasted countless days and months worrying about. After finding the guts to talk about my ordeal to people I trust, I've never looked back. I wish I'd had a book like this when I was going through the trauma because there's no help or advice about getting over it. The best thing was speaking up and having people around me who believed and supported me.

Ian
• • • • • • •

From early adolescence onward I was always seen as the black sheep of the family. No one told me why. I went from being a straight-A student to being a punk. I thought I was rebelling, but in fact I was responding to a sociopathic mother and an apathetic father.

From my teens I had hated my father for being aggressive and angry all the time and my mother for being weak and the victim. What I was not aware of at the time was how the situation was being played out and manipulated by my mother. I now recognize that my mother was the person with the problem, but it didn't seem so back then. She was so good at seeking pity and playing the victim. Yet in reality she was in control of the situation, and she had to be the center of attention.

When I was very young she used to dress me up in white suits (this *was* the early seventies!). I couldn't play with friends in case I got the clothes dirty. She would rather show me off to her friends as if I were a prized object. She never showed me affection, not even in private. Our father used to sleep during the day as he often worked night shifts. Our mother would tell me and my siblings not to talk loudly during the day in case it angered our father. As a consequence we became very afraid of him. All through my childhood and adolescence my mother would say we had no money, yet she was known for her extravagant clothes and expensive tastes. In fact, I remember her parading around in an expensive fur coat. Everything had to revolve around my mother and her wants. She controlled all aspects of family life, even though she acted hard done by.

My brother, my sister, and I were pawns in a horrible game between my parents. After many heated arguments between them, my father one day decided he had had enough of the situation. But instead of focusing his anger on my mother, he focused it on me. I admit that at fifteen I was rebelling against them. I no longer did everything the way my parents wanted and became less compliant, but I was not particularly wayward—quite the contrary. I was becoming increasingly withdrawn. In the end, my father told my mother she had to choose between him and me. She chose him. As a result, I was sent to live with my grandmother until I finished school.

Over the following two years I had periods of great instability. At one point I was destitute, homeless, and had to get food stamps. I was allowed occasional contact with my family, but this was controlled by my mother, who always warned me not to upset my father, brother, and sister. She continued to insist that I was the problem. Later I used my appearance as an act of rebellion. I became a punk. I looked aggressive, but underneath I was still a quiet and peaceable character. Then at nineteen I started my career. I wanted to help other people who might have experienced problems similar to mine. I moved to another city and trained as a psychiatric nurse. Other people's problems seemed, in general, a lot simpler than my own.

wary of others. Terrified of being abandoned on the one hand, and of being dominated on the other, they fluctuate between extremes of submissiveness and rebellion. This has been termed "sitting duck syndrome."[4] In the most extreme cases, survivors of childhood abuse may find themselves involved in the abuse of others, either in the role of passive bystander or, more rarely, as a perpetrator.

Assisting a child in overcoming the effects of abuse is a challenge, but children can and do overcome trauma. Helping children make sense of things by listening to them and acting on their behalf when necessary will make a lot of difference in their ability to recover from childhood trauma. Apathy should not be tolerated by society, and it is part of the problem. A recent, high-profile example of the way in which apathy itself can form part of the abuse is the many cases of child sexual abuse by priests within the Catholic Church, which began coming to light in the mid-1980s. Sadly, cases occurring over many decades have since been reported in numerous countries throughout the world. Much of the scandal focused on members of the church's hierarchy who didn't report allegations of abuse to the civil authorities. Rather, in many cases they reassigned the accused priests to other locations, where they continued to have contact with minors.

Sociopathic Relatives

Sociopathy unfortunately can be an entrenched problem within families. Siblings, grandparents, aunts, and uncles may have some degree of sociopathy, or a related condition like narcissism. Nor is it uncommon for the adult children of sociopaths, whether or not they are sociopathic themselves, to attract, and be attracted to, sociopathic partners. In this way the cycle of abuse is often transferred from one generation to the next. And sometimes sociopaths join forces, or pair up with others who have conditions of zero or limited empathy, such as malignant narcissism. When these types combine they make for a potent, and potentially lethal, mix. Such couplings can prove almost impossible to contend with.

However, there is some evidence that narcissistic behavior can diminish with age; for instance, abusive or otherwise difficult fathers sometimes settle down and become seemingly decent grandfathers. Sociopaths, on the other hand, rarely if ever improve significantly with age, though they may seemingly become more subdued owing to a reduction in the opportunities they have to inflict harm.

Family members of sociopaths often become targets of manipulation—wherein one is pitted against the other—with the consequence that the family is damaged by destructive elements within. More often than not other members of the family fall in line, taking on the roles and functions that suit the sociopath best. All too often, the empath—the family member who is more perceptive and sees the situation for what it is—becomes the target of family hostility, eventually ending up either walking away or being expelled from the family group. In this chapter and the previous one we have proposed ways to help people in such dramatic and painful circumstances, but additional support may be necessary.

Sociopaths often emotionally abuse their intimate partners. According to the U.S. Office on Women's Health in the U.S. Department of Health and Human Services, attempts to scare, isolate, or control a person are forms of abuse. They can affect the target's physical and emotional well-being, and they often are a sign that physical abuse will follow.

Women are more likely to suffer domestic abuse in the United States; men are also subject to domestic violence, but are less likely to be physically hurt. The U.S. Office on Violence Against Women (OVW) defines domestic violence as a "pattern of abusive behavior in any relationship that is used by one partner to gain or maintain power and control over another intimate partner." The definition adds that domestic violence "can happen to anyone regardless of race, age, sexual orientation, religion, or gender," and can take many forms, including physical abuse, sexual abuse, or emotional, economic, or psychological abuse.

Various Violence Against Women Acts have been passed by the U.S. Congress in an attempt to stem the problem. The Family Violence Prevention and Services Act (FVPSA) ensures the provision of federal funding to help victims of domestic violence and their dependent children by providing shelter and related help, offering violence prevention programs, and improving how service agencies work together in communities.[5]

As discussed above, domestic abuse is an issue not only for adults, but also for children and teenagers. Young people's formative years are difficult at best, but if they're in an abusive family situation, a lack of experience in relationships and issues with self-confidence can cause them to they feel they have nowhere to turn. Many sources of support are available (see Resources); because each person's circumstances differ, some forms of support are more helpful than others. Family therapy, for example, is unlikely to prove helpful when there is a sociopath in the family, because sociopaths do not respond constructively to therapy and may run rings around the therapist, however well qualified and experienced he or she is. On the other hand, the non-sociopathic members of the family or household may benefit from professional counseling; it may prove highly valuable to have someone outside the situation listen to their concerns.

But a word of caution: Even trained and experienced counselors and psychotherapists may not be fully in the know when it comes to the issue of sociopathic abuse. They may fail to appreciate the nuances of sociopathy and the abusive interactions that can occur in families with sociopathic members. Our advice is to ask prospective therapists about their experience working with families who've endured sociopathic abuse, and only to engage the therapist if you feel confident in his or her ability to work effectively with this complex family dynamic and to handle the situation well.

Since those with firsthand experience of sociopathic abuse have begun to promote awareness of sociopathy and its harms, a significant amount of help has become available and numerous support groups have been set up to assist survivors. However, these groups are intended for adults, *not* children, though young adults may also find them beneficial. At present, we are not aware of any groups that cater specifically to young children or teenagers. The issue of online support for children remains fraught with difficulties, a situation that acts as a deterrent to would-be groups and advocates, not least because it is vital to protect children from the risk of further abuse.

Laying Down the Law with Problem Grandparents and Other Family Members

If the sociopathic family member happens to be someone other than a parent, for example a grandparent, aunt, or uncle, then the situation can be equally problematic. Adults with sociopathic parents or siblings are likely to feel torn between their desire to protect their child from abuse and their relatives' and society's expectation that members of an extended family should have access to grandchildren, nieces, and nephews. Such parents also have to contend with their own memories of emotional, physical, or sexual abuse at the hands of their parents or siblings, which can set off alarm bells about abuse occurring to their own children. This situation may prove just too difficult for the parents to deal with and may deter them from allowing their children to have any kind of relationship with the sociopathic family member(s).

In the case of sociopathic grandparents it is fairly common for the parents to allow the grandparents to begin a relationship with their grandchildren, hoping that things will be different this time, but unfortunately this is rarely the case; sociopathy is a lifelong and untreatable disorder. If contact is maintained, however, even in a limited way, the children involved may eventually be torn apart by the grief of having to sever a relationship with the unhealthy family member. The parent is also likely to experience secondary trauma if her children are abused by other members of the family. She may end up feeling mortified at having done more harm than good by allowing the sociopath access to her children.

It is important that parents consider the pros and cons of letting other family members have contact with their children. In her helpful blog "Light's Blog," (at lightshouse.org; see Resources), Drew Keys suggests that the following questions be used to help guide the decision-making process. If the answer to any of the questions is "no," then a rule of no contact is probably safest and best:

- Is the previously abusive family member a very different person from the one you remember?
- Do you currently have a healthy, functional, and stable relationship with the family member?
- Does the family member respect your choices and boundaries as a parent?
- Does the family member follow your requests about how you want your children to be treated and to behave?
- Would you recommend your parent or other family member as babysitter to your best friend without any hesitation, and would you

feel comfortable giving your word that the family member would never harm your friend's child?

If you find it very difficult to make a decision of this nature, seek professional help, as other family members will not be neutral or objective. Professionals may include an adviser from the local child protection agency, a family therapist, or a family lawyer.

In 2000 the U.S. Supreme Court ruled that there is no such thing as "grandparents' rights."[6] State courts considering nonparent visitation petitions must apply "a presumption that fit parents act in the best interests of their children," and must give special weight to a fit parent's decision to deny nonparent visitation: "Choices [parents make] about the upbringing of children...are among associational rights...sheltered by the Fourteenth Amendment against the State's unwarranted usurpation, disregard, or disrespect." Grandparents may try to gain access to their grandchildren, but "fit" parents who have established no-contact boundaries may always block attempts to access their grandchildren. A similar principle applies in the United Kingdom.

What If You Suspect Your Child Has Sociopathic Traits?

Although many children of sociopathic parents are healthy and happy, unfortunately some people experience years of problems with their children. There may be a number of reasons for this: The sociopath may have abandoned the children and left the other parent to raise them alone; the children may have been used as pawns in the sociopathic parent's manipulation games; or—the worst scenario of all—the children may turn out to be sociopathic themselves. Here we turn to the issues facing the parents of sociopathic children.

Because sociopathy in children remains a mostly hidden problem, there are very few real-life case studies to draw upon. A few films and novels draw attention to the issue. Granted, these are works of fiction, not claiming to be based on real-life cases, but they allow us to glimpse the nature of the problem. The 1993 psychological thriller *The Good Son* was mostly panned. Critics thought the sociopathic child, Henry, was too unrealistic. Roger Ebert wrote, "This is a very evil little boy.... [W]hat rings false is that the Macaulay Culkin character isn't really a little boy at all.... His speech is much too sophisticated and ironic for that, and so is his reasoning and his cleverness.... [H]e seems more like a distasteful device by the filmmakers, who apparently think there is a market for glib one-liners by child sadists."[7] Nevertheless, for those who live in close proximity to a sociopathic child, the film, with the exception of its implausible ending, is not so far-fetched; in fact the main character's glibness, artificiality, and indifference are accurate depictions of real-life child sociopaths. Below is a passage of dialogue from the film. A twelve-year-old boy named Mark has gone to visit his aunt and uncle and cousins, including Henry, who is the same age. Henry begins showing signs of sociopathic behavior. He has thrown a plastic doll over a highway overpass into oncoming traffic, causing a massive pile-up:

Mark: Do you know what you did?

Henry: Hey, come on. We did it together.

Mark: You could've killed people…

Henry: …with your help…

Mark: Hey, I didn't know you were gonna do that!

Henry: I feel sorry for you, Mark. You just don't know how to have fun.

Mark: What?

Henry: It's because you're scared all the time. I know. I used to be scared too. But that was before I found out.

Mark: Found out what?

Henry: That once you realize you can do anything, you're free. You could fly. Nobody can touch you—nobody. Mark, don't be afraid to fly.

Mark: You're sick.

Child sociopathy is also the theme of the 2011 film *We Need to Talk about Kevin*. The story is told from the perspective of a mother, Eva, who is the "seeing" person (the empath) in the family, and who has a son named Kevin who is a sociopath. Throughout his life he has been detached and difficult. He does not bond with his mother and as a baby he cries incessantly, rebuffs her attempts at affection, and shows no interest in anything. While Kevin is still small, Eva's frustration with his intractability drives her to him throw against the wall, breaking his arm. Eva's husband dismisses her concerns, makes excuses for his son, gives Kevin a bow and arrow set, and teaches him archery. Kevin becomes an excellent marksman. There follows a series of disturbing "accidents" in the household. Whereas the mother blames Kevin, the father insists that Kevin is blameless. Since her earlier concerns were dismissed, the mother keeps to herself her intensifying fear of her son. The story culminates with Kevin plotting and executing multiple killings. The paradox is that no one other than his mother talks about Kevin or his disturbing behavior. No one "sees" the problem for what it is.

By the time a child with such tendencies (we hope not as extreme) reaches school age, he or she is already on the way to developing into a sociopath. She may interact well with school friends, but the signs of antisocial behavior are already there. Some children exert control over others by bullying them on the school playground while showing a different personality at home. They are therefore difficult to detect, a problem compounded by the fact that no psychiatrist or psychologist will label a child a sociopath because it is regarded only as a *potential* problem at that stage. Instead, if pushed, psychologists identify such children as having "conduct disorder" or "callous unemotional traits." But more often than not, these children are not identified or brought to the attention of mental health professionals at all. Some may be passed off as antisocial and eventually get caught up in the criminal justice system, especially sociopathic boys.

All children make mistakes and have times when they are aggressive, lie, and manipulate; such characteristics are part of human nature. But children with callous unemotional traits, conduct disorder, or sociopathy display behavior that is extreme. They are capable of acts of great harm carried out with intent, as witnessed in our example of James, the school bully. James showed no guilt about getting others to gang up on Sam, or attempting to end his "favorite" teacher's career. Such children exist and are not the stuff of fiction; many have significant problems with aggression and deceit and will manipulate their way out of situations. And, just like their adult counterparts, they seem to have no conscience about their actions or about the consequences that befall others.

Identifying Sociopathic Children

Recently doctors have performed fMRI scans of the brains of children with callous unemotional (CU) traits, focusing on an area of the brain called the amygdala, where fear and negative emotions appear to be processed. In one study scientists showed children pictures of other people in emotionally distressing situations. Typically children have a strong amygdala response to other people's distress; however, in this study it was found that children with CU traits showed no discernible amygdala response on fMRI scans when they observed other people in distressing situations. This is the first time such a study has been done involving children. It reflects what has been found in many other studies carried out on adult sociopaths, and the findings are changing researchers' perception of sociopathy. Some scientists now believe these traits result from an underarousal of the amygdala in the children's brains.[8]

Most of us learn to care about how other people feel by seeing emotion and fear in them, which causes our own discomfort. If you don't feel discomfort or fear yourself, and you don't notice it in other people, you are highly unlikely to develop the higher-order human functions of empathy and moral conscience. As we stated in Chapter 1, sociopaths recognize that other people have emotions and use them to their advantage, but they don't feel much themselves. Antisocial children with CU traits appear to be disconnected from other people's feelings, just like adult sociopaths. Identifying children with these characteristics early and getting them into treatment is crucial. By the time such children reach puberty, it's often too late and they are untreatable.

So what are the warning signs? The Macdonald triad, proposed by J. M. Macdonald in 1963 and also known as the triad of sociopathy, is a set of three behavioral characteristics—animal cruelty, obsession with fire setting, and persistent bedwetting (past the age of five)—originally thought to be associated with later violent tendencies. However, this particular combination of behaviors has not been properly validated, and the characterization has been more or less debunked. Today, younger children whose disruptive and aggressive behavior takes place within the home but whose problem behaviors do not meet the criteria for conduct disorder may be diagnosed as having what's known as oppositional defiant disorder.

The key features present in older children with conduct disorder or high CU traits vary in intensity and breadth, but hallmark tendencies include a lack of conscience, lack of empathy, and lying and manipulative behav-

it is indicative of your increased independence. Many people feel a newfound sense of freedom and confidence, and a greater awareness of "self." The end stage of recovery is a time to be bold, a time to take risks and follow your instincts. It may involve lots of unexpected changes, but eventually, with any luck, balance will be restored.

When it comes to developing new relationships and friendships, someone betrayed in the ways discussed in this book may find him- or herself less trusting than before. The degree of mistrust will vary according to your personality as well as to the nature of the betrayal. But the crux of the matter is that under normal circumstances, if a betrayal has occurred, the wrongdoer would be expected to admit that he or she has inflicted a deep hurt. For people who have been traumatized by a sociopath, this possibility is denied them. An apology will never be forthcoming—not a genuine one, at any rate. So the person in recovery must contend with an inadequate ending to the whole sorry saga. With a sociopath there is no satisfying end point or sense of closure.

Dealing with Stigma

The end stage of recovery may be a lone journey, but it is not one to be taken wearing a badge of shame. You must learn to walk tall, to cast off the stigma and social disapproval of having experienced trauma at the hands of another human being.

The central dilemma for people recovering from sociopathic abuse, according to Judith Herman in her landmark book *Trauma and Recovery,* is whether to be vociferous or to keep quiet about their past situation.[1] One way of dealing with any stigma is to quietly get on with your life and not let others' views bother you. Another is to confront the stigma head on. It is up to each individual to deal with the issue as best suits him or her. For many adult children who were abused by a sociopathic parent, getting over the shame of child abuse is the biggest challenge, one that may be met by not letting the experience adversely affect the rest of your life. It requires that you learn to love yourself and accept your past experiences, good and bad. Hopefully, at some point, those nearing the end stages of recovery will reach a place where they recognize that while they were a victim of abuse as a child, they are surviving that abuse as an adult and managing their lives well.

Tackling the social stigma of sociopathic abuse can be part of the later stages of recovery. Campaigning about the hidden harms of sociopathic abuse is one way of going about this. The self-help ethos of many recovery groups is not only an effective way of reaching out and supporting marginalized individuals and groups, but is also beneficial to society as a whole. The act of coming together and taking collective action raises the profile of the issue and alters public perceptions. Moreover, by supporting campaigning groups or being vocal about sociopathic abuse, the abused person can come to appreciate his own journey and his movement through the process of recovery. For some, helping to bring the issue to the public's awareness is an absolute necessity, a way of breaking the silence and challenging the apathy in society. What often stops people from speaking out about the problem is the shame inflicted upon them by others.

Jeremy Rifkin, author of *The Empathic Civilization,* describes a shaming culture as one that "pretends to adhere to the highest possible standards of moral perfection."[2] Historically, shaming cultures have been the most aggressive and violent because "they lock up the empathic impulse." We see this in the way that women are sometimes said to be "asking for it" when they are sexually assaulted, for example. This kind of response stops us from empathizing with their plight. Breaking down the stigma requires individual and collective action to expose the harms of antisocial behavior. Thereafter, each of us needs to contribute to a culture in which empathy exists as a prized virtue with the potential to transform human beings into individuals with high levels of interpersonal and emotional intelligence. Empathic responses can be learned through cultural transmission. Parents, teachers, and other adults of all ages should be the next generation's enlightened witnesses, helping children to make emotional connections and to advance positive and healing interactions.

Rifkin highlights a study that is worth recounting here. Having observed the behavior of adolescent elephants in an animal park in South Africa, zoologists noted that for unknown reasons the elephants had begun to taunt and kill other animals. The zoologists recalled that, years earlier, they had culled the adult male elephants to ease overcrowding. They decided to bring back two older male elephants. It transpired that the reintroduction of the older elephants stopped the younger elephants from behaving in an antisocial manner. Rifkin suggests that young people, like the elephants in the study, require adult role models to set the boundaries around social behavior.[3] It is up to every one of us to set standards of social behavior and maintain them by establishing clear boundaries.

Getting a child to understand how her behavior affects other children and how she would feel if the same misbehavior were enacted on her requires a parent or adult with empathy and a well-developed conscience. The adult's role is to act as the child's guide, helping the child reflect on her own behavior, feel remorse, and prepare to make reparation for her misdemeanor. Through this process, positive human attributes such as altruism and empathy are advanced. The benefits are likely to be substantial. As internationally renowned professor of psychiatry Stanley Greenspan argues, "Mental health requires a feeling of connectedness with humanity…which in turn requires a well-developed sense of empathy."[4]

◆ ◆ ◆ ◆ ◆ ◆

Appendix:
The Empathy Quotient (EQ) Test

The Empathy Quotient, devised by Simon Baron-Cohen and reproduced here with his permission, is intended to measure how easily you pick up on other people's feelings and how strongly you are affected by others' feelings. If you wish to take the test, read each of the sixty statements very carefully and rate how strongly you agree or disagree with them by circling your answer. If using the test reproduced in the table, calculate your EQ score using the points system explained at the end of the questionnaire. Or you can perform the test online by visiting glennrowe .net/BaronCohen/EmpathyQuotient/EmpathyQuotient.aspx.

There are no right or wrong answers or trick questions. We advise you not to take this test too seriously—it is provided here simply for your interest. A child version of the Empathy Quotient is available in Baron-Cohen, *Zero Degrees of Empathy: A New Theory of Human Cruelty* (2011), London: Allen Lane/Penguin Books, Appendix 1, 135–39.

The Empathy Quotient (EQ) test

1. I can easily tell if someone else wants to enter a conversation.

   strongly agree | slightly agree | slightly disagree | strongly disagree

2. I prefer animals to humans.

   strongly agree | slightly agree | slightly disagree | strongly disagree

3. I try to keep up with the current trends and fashions.

   strongly agree | slightly agree | slightly disagree | strongly disagree

4. I find it difficult to explain to others things that I understand easily, when they don't understand it [the] first time.

strongly agree | slightly agree | slightly disagree | strongly disagree

5. I dream most nights.

strongly agree | slightly agree | slightly disagree | strongly disagree

6. I really enjoy caring for other people.

strongly agree | slightly agree | slightly disagree | strongly disagree

7. I try to solve my own problems rather than discussing them with others.

strongly agree | slightly agree | slightly disagree | strongly disagree

8. I find it hard to know what to do in a social situation.

strongly agree | slightly agree | slightly disagree | strongly disagree

9. I am at my best first thing in the morning.

strongly agree | slightly agree | slightly disagree | strongly disagree

10. People often tell me that I went too far in driving my point home in a discussion.

strongly agree | slightly agree | slightly disagree | strongly disagree

11. It doesn't bother me too much if I am late meeting a friend.

strongly agree | slightly agree | slightly disagree | strongly disagree

12. Friendships and relationships are just too difficult, so I tend not to bother with them.

strongly agree | slightly agree | slightly disagree | strongly disagree

13. I would never break a law, no matter how minor.

strongly agree | slightly agree | slightly disagree | strongly disagree

14. I often find it difficult to judge if something is rude or polite.

strongly agree | slightly agree | slightly disagree | strongly disagree

15. In a conversation, I tend to focus on my own thoughts rather than on what my listener might be thinking.

strongly agree | slightly agree | slightly disagree | strongly disagree

16. I prefer practical jokes to verbal humor.

strongly agree | slightly agree | slightly disagree | strongly disagree

17. I live life for today rather than for the future.

strongly agree | slightly agree | slightly disagree | strongly disagree

18. When I was a child, I enjoyed cutting up worms to see what would happen.

strongly agree | slightly agree | slightly disagree | strongly disagree

19. I can pick up quickly if someone says one thing but means another.

strongly agree | slightly agree | slightly disagree | strongly disagree

20. I tend to have very strong opinions about morality.

strongly agree | slightly agree | slightly disagree | strongly disagree

21. It is hard for me to see why some things upset people so much.

strongly agree | slightly agree | slightly disagree | strongly disagree

22. I find it easy to put myself in somebody else's shoes.

strongly agree | slightly agree | slightly disagree | strongly disagree

23. I think good manners are the most important thing a parent can teach their child.

strongly agree | slightly agree | slightly disagree | strongly disagree

24. I like to do things on the spur of the moment.

strongly agree | slightly agree | slightly disagree | strongly disagree

25. I am good at predicting how someone will feel.

strongly agree | slightly agree | slightly disagree | strongly disagree

26. I am quick to spot when someone in a group is feeling awkward or uncomfortable.

strongly agree | slightly agree | slightly disagree | strongly disagree

27. If I say something that someone else is offended by, I think that that's their problem, not mine.

strongly agree | slightly agree | slightly disagree | strongly disagree

28. If anyone asked me if I liked their haircut, I would reply truthfully, even if I didn't like it.

strongly agree | slightly agree | slightly disagree | strongly disagree

29. I can't always see why someone should have felt offended by a remark.

strongly agree | slightly agree | slightly disagree | strongly disagree

30. People often tell me that I am very unpredictable.

strongly agree | slightly agree | slightly disagree | strongly disagree

31. I enjoy being the center of attention at any social gathering.

strongly agree | slightly agree | slightly disagree | strongly disagree

32. Seeing people cry doesn't really upset me.

strongly agree | slightly agree | slightly disagree | strongly disagree

33. I enjoy having discussions about politics.

strongly agree | slightly agree | slightly disagree | strongly disagree

34. I am very blunt, which some people take to be rudeness, even though this is unintentional.

strongly agree | slightly agree | slightly disagree | strongly disagree

35. I don't tend to find social situations confusing.

strongly agree | slightly agree | slightly disagree | strongly disagree

36. Other people tell me I am good at understanding how they are feeling and what they are thinking.

strongly agree | slightly agree | slightly disagree | strongly disagree

37. When I talk to people, I tend to talk about their experiences rather than my own.

strongly agree | slightly agree | slightly disagree | strongly disagree

38. It upsets me to see an animal in pain.

strongly agree | slightly agree | slightly disagree | strongly disagree

39. I am able to make decisions without being influenced by people's feelings.

strongly agree | slightly agree | slightly disagree | strongly disagree

40. I can't relax until I have done everything I had planned to do that day.

    strongly agree | slightly agree | slightly disagree | strongly disagree

41. I can easily tell if someone else is interested or bored with what I am saying.

    strongly agree | slightly agree | slightly disagree | strongly disagree

42. I get upset if I see people suffering on news programmes.

    strongly agree | slightly agree | slightly disagree | strongly disagree

43. Friends usually talk to me about their problems as they say that I am very understanding.

    strongly agree | slightly agree | slightly disagree | strongly disagree

44. I can sense if I am intruding, even if the other person doesn't tell me.

    strongly agree | slightly agree | slightly disagree | strongly disagree

45. I often start new hobbies but quickly become bored with them and move on to something else.

    strongly agree | slightly agree | slightly disagree | strongly disagree

46. People sometimes tell me that I have gone too far with teasing.

    strongly agree | slightly agree | slightly disagree | strongly disagree

47. I would be too nervous to go on a big rollercoaster.

    strongly agree | slightly agree | slightly disagree | strongly disagree

48. Other people often say that I am insensitive, though I don't always see why.

    strongly agree | slightly agree | slightly disagree | strongly disagree

49. If I see a stranger in a group, I think it is up to them to make an effort to join in.

    strongly agree | slightly agree | slightly disagree | strongly disagree

50. I usually stay emotionally detached when watching a film.

    strongly agree | slightly agree | slightly disagree | strongly disagree

51. I like to be very organized in day to day life and often make lists of the chores I have to do.

strongly agree | slightly agree | slightly disagree | strongly disagree

52. I can tune into how someone else feels rapidly and intuitively.

strongly agree | slightly agree | slightly disagree | strongly disagree

53. I don't like to take risks.

strongly agree | slightly agree | slightly disagree | strongly disagree

54. I can easily work out what another person might want to talk about.

strongly agree | slightly agree | slightly disagree | strongly disagree

55. I can tell if someone is masking their true emotion.

strongly agree | slightly agree | slightly disagree | strongly disagree

56. Before making a decision I always weigh up the pros and cons.

strongly agree | slightly agree | slightly disagree | strongly disagree

57. I don't consciously work out the rules of social situations.

strongly agree | slightly agree | slightly disagree | strongly disagree

58. I am good at predicting what someone will do.

strongly agree | slightly agree | slightly disagree | strongly disagree

59. I tend to get emotionally involved with a friend's problems.

strongly agree | slightly agree | slightly disagree | strongly disagree

60. I can usually appreciate the other person's viewpoint, even if I don't agree with it.

strongly agree | slightly agree | slightly disagree | strongly disagree

The EQ test was devised by Professor Simon Baron-Cohen and Dr. Sally Wheelwright and first appeared in the following academic journals: *Journal of Autism and Developmental Disorders* (2004) 34, 163; *Psychological Medicine* (2004) 34, 911.

The EQ test is a questionnaire that is completed by adults (over sixteen years old) or by their parent (if using the child or adolescent version of this test). It reveals individual differences in empathy, both "cognitive" and "affective" empathy. It can be used for screening purposes but is not diagnostic. A low score indicates low empathy.

The EQ test is provided "as is," and the creators and the university make no warranties of any kind, either express or implied, concerning the EQ. The EQ is provided for research use only and should not be used to inform clinical decisions. Any commercial use of the EQ is prohibited without the prior express written permission from the creators and the university.

How to Determine Your EQ Score

- Score **two points** for each of the following items if you answered "strongly agree" or **one point** if you answered "slightly agree": 1, 6, 19, 22, 25, 26, 35, 36, 37, 38, 41, 42, 43, 44, 52, 54, 55, 57, 58, 59, 60.

- Score **two points** for each of the following items if you answered "strongly disagree" or **one point** if you answered "slightly disagree": 4, 8, 10, 11, 12, 14, 15, 18, 21, 27, 28, 29, 32, 34, 39, 46, 48, 49, 50.

  All other questions are not scored.

What Your Score Means

On average, most women score about 47 and most men about 42. Most people with Asperger syndrome or high-functioning autism score about 20.

0–32: You have a lower than average ability for understanding how other people feel and responding appropriately.

33–52: You have an average ability for understanding how other people feel and responding appropriately. You know how to treat people with care and sensitivity.

53–63: You have an above average ability for understanding how other people feel and responding appropriately. You know how to treat people with care and sensitivity.

64–80: You have a very high ability for understanding how other people feel and responding appropriately. You know how to treat people with care and sensitivity.

Notes

Introduction

1. K. L. Barry et al., "Conduct Disorder and Antisocial Personality in Adult Primary Care Patients," *Journal of Family Practice* 45, no. 2 (2007), 15–18. There is also an earlier study: J. F. Samuels et al., "DSM-III Personality Disorders in the Community," *American Journal of Psychiatry* 151, no. 7 (1994): 1055–62. This gave a prevalence estimate of 5.9 percent of all types of personality disorders in adults in the community.
2. P. Babiak and R. D. Hare, *Snakes in Suits* (New York: Collins, 2006).
3. J. Clarke, *Working with Monsters: How to Identify and Protect Yourself from the Workplace Psychopath* (Sydney, Australia: Random House, 2009).
4. J. W. Coid et al., "Prevalence and Correlates of Psychopathic Traits in the Household Population of Great Britain," *International Journal of Law and Psychiatry* 32 (2009): 265–73.
5. R. D. Hare, *Without Conscience: The Disturbing World of the Psychopaths Among Us* (New York: Guilford Press, 1993), 83–96.

Chapter 1: Everyday Sociopaths

1. The term "narcissistic" derives from Narcissus, the figure from Greek mythology known for his beauty. Narcissus was exceptionally proud and vain. Nemesis (the goddess of divine retribution or revenge) recognized this characteristic in him and lured Narcissus to a pool, where he saw his own reflection in the water. Not realizing it was an image of himself, he soon fell in love with it, but unable to leave the beauty of his own reflection, he died.
2. P. Pinel, *A Treatise on Insanity*, trans. D. D. Davies (New York: Hafner, 1806. Republished in 1962), 150–56.

3. J. C. Pritchard, *A Treatise on Insanity and Other Disorders Affecting the Mind* (London: Sherwood, Gilbert and Piper, 1835). He also published *On the Different Forms of Insanity in Relation to Jurisprudence* (London: Hippolyte Bailliere, 1847).

4. H. Cleckley, *The Mask of Sanity: An Attempt to Reinterpret the So-Called Psychopathic Personality* (St. Louis, MO: C.V. Mosby, 1976), vii.

5. R. D. Hare, *Without Conscience* (New York: Guilford Press, 1993), 23–4.

6. S. Baron-Cohen, *Zero Degrees of Empathy: A New Theory of Human Cruelty* (London: Allen Lane/Penguin Books, 2011). A full explanation of the empathy circuit can be found on pp. 19–28.

7. The emerging science on empathy is effectively conveyed in C. Keysers, *The Empathic Brain: How the Understanding of Mirror Neurons Changes our Understanding of Human Nature* (Amsterdam: Social Brain Press, 2011).

Chapter 2: A Profile of the Sociopath

1. M. Stout, *The Sociopath Next Door* (New York: Broadway Books, 2005).

2. Passive-aggressive behavior takes many forms but can generally be described as nonverbal aggression. It presents when one person is angry with another but does not or cannot tell them. Instead of communicating honestly when they feel upset, annoyed, irritated, or disappointed, such people shut off verbally, give angry looks, or become obstructive or sulky. It can either be covert (concealed and hidden) or overt (blatant and obvious).

3. A. Harrn, "What Is Passive Aggressive Behavior?" Counselling Directory, 2011. http://www.counselling-directory.org.uk/counsellor-articles/what-is-passive-aggressive-behavior.

4. H. B. Braiker, *Who's Pulling Your Strings? How to Break the Cycle of Manipulation* (New York: McGraw-Hill, 2004).

5. P. Babiak and R. Hare, *Snakes in Suits: When Psychopaths Go to Work* (New York: HarperCollins, 2006).

6. For more about pathological lying see C. C. Dike (2008), "Pathological Lying: Symptom or Disease?" *Psychiatric Times* 25, no. 7 (2008). http://www.psychiatrictimes.com/print/article/10168/1162950 (accessed .

7. S. Baron-Cohen, *Zero Degrees of Empathy: A New Theory of Human Cruelty* (London: Allen Lane/Penguin Books, 2011).

8. M. K. F. Kreis and D. J. Cooke, "Capturing the Psychopathic Female: A Prototypicality Analysis of the Comprehensive Assessment of Psychopathic

Personality (CAPP) Across Gender," *Behavioral Sciences and the Law* 29 (2011): 634–48. Also C. Logan, "La Femme Fatale: The Female Psychopath in Fiction and Clinical Practice," *Mental Health Review Journal* 16, no. 3 (2011): 118–27.

9. T. L. Nicholls et al., "Psychopathy in Women: A Review of Its Clinical Usefulness for Assessing Risk for Aggression and Criminality," *Behavioral Sciences and the Law* 23, no. 6 (2005): 779–802.

Chapter 3: Sociopathic Interactions

1. "The Perils of Obedience," *Harper's Magazine*. Available at www.age-of-the -sage.org/psychology/milgram_perils_authority_1974.html. The article was abridged and adapted from Stanley Milgram, *Obedience to Authority, 1974*.

2. *The Wave* (German: *Die Welle*, 2008). Dir. Dennis Gansel.

3. B. Klink, "'Third Wave' Presents Inside Look into Fascism: The Catamount" 11, no. 14 (21 April 1967): 3.

4. L. Gibson, "Mirrored Emotions," *University of Chicago Magazine* 98 (2006): 4.

5. P. Salovey and J. D. Mayer, "Emotional Intelligence," *Imagination, Cognition, and Personality* 9 (1990): 185–211.

6. C. Steiner and P. Perry, *Achieving Emotional Literacy* (London: Bloomsbury, 1997), 11.

7. C. Louis de Canonville, *The Effects of Gaslighting in Narcissistic Victim Syndrome*, 2011. Available online at narcissisticbehavior.net/the-effects-of-gas lighting-in-narcissistic-victim-syndrome.

8. R. Stern, *The Gaslight Effect: How to Spot and Survive the Hidden Manipulation Others Use to Control Your Life* (New York: Morgan Road Books, 2007).

Chapter 4: Coping in the Aftermath of a Destructive Relationship

1. M. Stout, *The Sociopath Next Door* (New York: Broadway Books, 2005).

2. J. Bradshaw, *Healing the Shame That Binds You* (Florida: Health Communications, 1988).

3. A. Miller (2007), *The Drama of the Gifted Child: The Search for the True Self*, rev. ed. (New York: Basic Books, 2007).

4. E. Kübler-Ross and D. Kessler, *On Grief and Grieving: Finding the Meaning of Grief Through the Five Stages of Loss* (New York: Scribner, 2007).

5. The tips and strategies in this chapter are adapted from a guide on anger

management by L. Garratt and P. Blackburn, Newcastle Primary Care Trust, Newcastle, U.K., (2007).

6. Available at www.mind.org.uk.

7. J. Lewis Herman, "Complex PTSD: A Syndrome in Survivors of Prolonged and Repeated Trauma," *Journal of Traumatic Stress* 5, no. 3 (1992): 377–91.

8. B. P. R. Gersons, "Coping with the Aftermath of Trauma," *British Medical Journal* 330, (2005): 1038.

9. L. Shengold, *Soul Murder: The Effects of Childhood Abuse and Deprivation* (New Haven: Yale University Press, 1989).

Chapter 5: Establishing Boundaries and Regaining Control of Your Life

1. U.S. Equal Employment Opportunity Commission, "Harassment," http://www.eeoc.gov/laws/practices/harassment.cfm (accessed 18 October 2013).

2. Wikipedia, "Anti-bullying Legislation," http://en.wikipedia.org/wiki/Anti -bullying_legislation (accessed 18 October 2013).

3. A. Miller, *Banished Knowledge: Facing Childhood Injuries* (New York: Anchor Press, 1997).

4. G. A. Marlatt and J. R. Gordon, *Relapse Prevention: Maintenance Strategies in the Treatment of Addictive Behaviors* (New York: Guilford Press, 1985).

5. B. J. Fogg, *The Behavior Model* (Persuasive Technology Lab: Stanford University, 2009).

Chapter 6: Handling Complex Family Situations

1. R. D. Hare, *Without Conscience: The Disturbing World of the Psychopaths Among Us* (New York: Guilford Press, 1993).

2. A. Miller, *The Body Never Lies: The Lingering Effects of Cruel Parenting* (New York: W.W. Norton, 2005).

3. J. Lewis Herman, "Complex PTSD: A Syndrome in Survivors of Prolonged and Repeated Trauma," *Journal of Traumatic Stress* 5, no. 3 (1992): 377–91.

4. R. P. Kluft, "Incest and Subsequent Revictimization: The Case of Therapist–Patient Sexual Exploitation, with a Description of the Sitting Duck Syndrome," in *Incest-Related Syndromes of Adult Psychopathology* (Washington, DC: American Psychiatric Press, 1990), 263–89.

5. Wikipedia, "Family Violence Prevention and Services Act," http://en.wiki pedia.org/wiki/Family_Violence_Prevention_and_Services_Act (accessed

18 October 2013); Office of Women's Health, U.S. Department of Health and Human Services, "Violence Against Women—Emotional Abuse," http:// www.womenshealth.gov/violence-against-women/types-of-violence/emo tional-abuse.html (accessed 18 October 2013).

6. U.S. Supreme Court Case, *Troxel vs. Granville* (2000).

7. R. Ebert, "The Good Son," *Chicago Sun-Times* (24 September 1993).

8. M. R. Dadds and T. Rhodes, "Aggression in Young Children with Concur-rent Callous–Unemotional Traits: Can the Neurosciences Inform Progress and Innovation in Treatment Approaches?" *Philosophical Transactions of the Royal Society B: Biological Sciences* 363, no. 1503 (2008): 2567–76.

9. D. S. Pasalich et al., "Do Callous-Unemotional Traits Moderate the Relative Importance of Parental Coercion Versus Warmth in Child Conduct Prob-lems? An Observational Study," *Journal of Child Psychology and Psychiatry and Allied Disciplines* 52, no. 12 (2011): 1308–15.

Chapter 7: End-Stage Recovery

1. J. L. Herman, *Trauma and Recovery* (New York: Basic Books, 1997).

2. J. Rifkin, *The Empathic Civilization: The Race to Global Consciousness in a World in Crisis* (Cambridge, UK: Polity, 2009), 121.

3. Ibid., 87–88.

4. S. Greenspan, *The Growth of the Mind: And the Endangered Origins of Intelli-gence* (Reading, MA: Addison Wesley, 1997), 193.

Resources

United States

Alliance for Non-Custodial Parents Rights
www.ancpr.com
Provides information on various issues, including parental rights. Their *Winning Strategies Handbook* is available to download.

American Coalition for Fathers and Children
(800) 978-3237 for general inquiries (very busy switchboard); www.acfc.org

Domestic Abuse Helpline for Men and Women (DAHMW)
(888) 7HELPLINE (888-743-5754); www.dahmw.org

Equal Employment Opportunity Commission (EEOC)
(800) 669-4000; www.eeoc.gov
The agency charged with enforcing federal laws that make it illegal to discriminate against a job applicant or an employee. The laws apply to all types of work situations, including hiring, firing, promotions, harassment, training, wages, and benefits.

Find a Psychologist
www.findapsychologist.org/about.html
Online directory listing of eleven thousand psychologists and their credentials.

National Child Abuse Hotline
(800) 4-A-CHILD (800-422-4453); www.childhelp.org

National Domestic Violence Hotline
(800) 799-SAFE (7233); www.thehotline.org
Provides advice, support, and referral to battered women's shelters in all areas of the country.

Separated Parenting Access and Resource Center
www.deltabravo.net
A nonprofit, website-based organization with the aim of enabling children of divorcees to have access to both parents.

Canada

National Domestic Violence Hotline
(800) 363-9010

Post-Traumatic Stress Disorder (PTSD) Association
www.ptsdassociation.com
Contact available only by e-mail via the website. Provides resources such as links to services, ongoing research, articles, and strategies for recognizing and coping with PTSD.

International

International Directory of Domestic Violence Agencies
www.hotpeachpages.net
A global list of helplines and crisis centers.

Other Online Resources

Aftermath: Surviving Psychopathy Foundation
www.aftermath-surviving-psychopathy.org
Contact by e-mail via the website, or write to PO Box 267, Yorkville, IL 60560.

Anxiety Help Center
www.helpguide.org/topics/anxiety.htm
A site run by a nonprofit group; no personal advice but useful resources are provided.

Bully OnLine
www.bullyonline.org
The world's largest resource on workplace bullying and related issues.

The Culture of Empathy
www.cultureofempathy.com
A portal for resources about the values of empathy and compassion worldwide.

EMDR Institute Inc.
www.emdr.com
Eye Movement Desensitization and Reprocessing is a treatment approach for trauma victims.

Emotional Health Help Center
www.helpguide.org/topics/emotional_health.htm

Estranged Stories
www.estrangedstories.com
A site where people experiencing estrangement from their family can find support.

Facebook
www.facebook.com
Search using the term "sociopath," "narcissist," or "psychopath" for survivor support groups. Some groups are closed and you have to request to join to become a member, while others are open forums available to anyone.

Light's Blog at Light's House
www.lightshouse.org/lights-blog

Stress Help Center
www.helpguide.org/topics/stress.htm

Books

Anderson, D. *Love Fraud: How Marriage to a Sociopath Fulfilled My Spiritual Plan.* New Jersey: Anderly Publishing, 2010.

Babiak, P., and R. D. Hare. *Snakes in Suits: When Psychopaths Go to Work.* New York: Collins, 2006.

Baron-Cohen, S. *Zero Degrees of Empathy: A New Theory of Human Cruelty.* London: Allen Lane/Penguin Books, 2011.

Behary, W. T. *Disarming the Narcissist: Surviving and Thriving with the Self-Absorbed.* Oakland, CA: New Harbinger, 2008.

Bentley, B. *A Dance with the Devil: A True Story of Marriage to a Psychopath.* New York: Berkley Books, 2008.

Bradshaw, J. *Healing the Shame That Binds You.* Deerfield Beach, FL: Health Communications, 1988.

Bradshaw, J. *The Family: A New Way of Creating Solid Self-Esteem.* Deerfield Beach, FL: Health Communications, 1996.

Braiker, H. B. *Who's Pulling Your Strings? How to Break the Cycle of Manipulation and Regain Control of Your Life.* New York: McGraw-Hill, 2004.

Brown, N. W. *The Destructive Narcissistic Pattern.* Westport, CT: Praeger, 1998.

———. *Children of the Self-Absorbed.* Oakland, CA: New Harbinger, 2001.

Buttafuoco, M. J. *Getting It Through My Thick Skull.* Deerfield Beach, FL: Health Communications, 2009.

Clarke, J. *Working with Monsters: How to Identify and Protect Yourself from the Workplace Psychopath.* Sydney, Australia: Random House, 2009.

Covey, S. K. *In the Arms of a Sociopath.* Frederick, MD: PublishAmerica, 2009.

Daynes, K., and J. Fellows. *The Devil You Know: Looking Out for the Psycho in Your Life.* London: Coronet, 2011.

de Becker, G. *The Gift of Fear: Survival Signals That Protect Us from Violence.* Canada: Little, Brown, 1997.

Donaldson-Pressman, S., and R. D. Pressman. *Narcissistic Family: Diagnosis and Treatment.* New York: Wiley & Sons, 1997.

Dryden, W. *How to Accept Yourself.* London: Sheldon Press, 1999.

Engel, B. *The Jekyll and Hyde Syndrome: What to Do If Someone in Your Life Has a Dual Personality—or If You Do.* New Jersey: John Wiley & Sons, 2007.

Evans, P. *Controlling People: How to Recognize, Understand, and Deal with People Who Try to Control You.* Canada: Adams Media, 2002.

Faulks, S. *Engleby.* London: Vintage, 2008.

Forward, S. *Toxic Parents: Overcoming Their Hurtful Legacy and Reclaiming Your Life.* New York: Bantam, 1989.

Golomb, E. *Trapped in the Mirror.* New York: Morrow, 1992.

Gootnick, I. *Why You Behave in Ways You Hate: And What You Can Do About It.* Roseville, CA: Penmarin Books, 1997.

Greenspan, S. L., with B. L. Benderly. *The Growth of the Mind and the Endangered Origins of Intelligence.* Reading, MA: Addison-Wesley, 1997.

Hare, R. D. *Without Conscience: The Disturbing World of the Psychopaths Among Us.* New York: Guilford Press, 1993.

Herbert, C., and A. Westmore. *Overcoming Traumatic Stress: A Self-Help Guide Using Cognitive Behavioral Techniques.* London: Constable & Robinson, 2008.

Keysers, C. *The Empathic Brain: How the Understanding of Mirror Neurons Changes Our Understanding of Human Nature.* Amsterdam: Social Brain Press, 2011.

Lerner, R. *The Object of My Affection Is in My Reflection: Narcissists and Their Relationships.* Deerfield Beach, FL: Health Communications, 2009.

Lewis Herman, J. *Trauma and Recovery: The Aftermath of Violence—from Domestic Abuse to Political Terror.* New York: Basic Books, 1997.

McBride, K. *Will I Ever Be Good Enough? Healing the Daughters of Narcissistic Mothers.* New York: Simon & Schuster, 2008.

Miller, A. *For Your Own Good: Hidden Cruelty in Childrearing and the Roots of Violence.* New York: Farrar, Straus & Giroux, 1990.

———. *Banished Knowledge: Facing Childhood Injuries.* New York: Anchor Press, 1997.

———. *Thou Shalt Not Be Aware: Society's Betrayal of the Child.* New York: Farrar, Straus and Giroux, 1998.

———. *The Truth Will Set You Free: Overcoming Emotional Blindness and Finding Your True Adult Self.* New York: Basic Books, 2001.

———. *The Body Never Lies: The Lingering Effects of Cruel Parenting.* New York: W. W. Norton, 2005.

———. *The Drama of the Gifted Child: The Search for the True Self,* rev. ed. New York: Basic Books, 2007.

Payson, E. D. *The Wizard of Oz and Other Narcissists: Coping with the One-Way Relationship in Work, Love and Family.* Royal Oak, MI: Julian Day, 2002.

Rifkin, J. *The Empathic Civilization: The Race to Global Consciousness in a World in Crisis.* Cambridge, UK: Polity Press, 2009.

Roan, C. *The Sociopath and Me.* Bloomington, IN: Trafford Publishing, 2011.

Ronson, J. *Out of the Ordinary: True Tales of Everyday Craziness.* London: Picador, 2006.

———. *What I Do: More True Tales of Everyday Craziness.* London: Picador, 2007.

———. *The Psychopath Test.* London: Picador, 2011.

Schiraldi, G. *The Post-Traumatic Stress Disorder Sourcebook: A Guide to Healing, Recovery and Growth.* New York: McGraw-Hill, 2009.

Silberschatz, G. *Transformative Relationships.* New York: Taylor & Francis, 2005.

Sichel, M. *Healing from Family Rifts.* New York: McGraw-Hill, 2004.

Simon, G. *In Sheep's Clothing.* Little Rock: Parkhurst Brothers, 1996.

Stern, R. *The Gaslight Effect: How to Spot and Survive the Hidden Manipulation Others Use to Control Your Life.* New York: Morgan Road Books, 2007.

Stout, M. *The Sociopath Next Door.* New York: Broadway Books, 2005.

Walker, M. *Surviving Secrets.* Buckingham: Open University Press, 2000.

Films

The Good Son (1993). American thriller directed by Joseph Ruben, written by English novelist Ian McEwan, and starring Macaulay Culkin and Elijah Wood.

The Wave (German: *Die Welle*, 2008). A German film directed by Dennis Gansel and based on the book *The Wave*, which was inspired by the social experiment the Third Wave.

We Need to Talk about Kevin (2011). British-American film adapted and directed by Lynne Ramsay from American author Lionel Shriver's 2003 novel of the same name.

Index

About the Authors

DR. JANE MCGREGOR is a freelance writer and trainer, and a part-time lecturer at the School of Health Sciences, University of Nottingham, U.K. She received a PhD in public health from the London School of Hygiene and Tropical Medicine, funded by the Wellcome Trust. Jane worked in the National Health Service and in the voluntary sector for many years, mostly in the field of addiction treatment, and she has published widely in this area.

TIM MCGREGOR is a freelance consultant, writer, and trainer. He has been a mental-health practitioner for many years and has worked in both the National Health Service and the U.K. voluntary sector, most recently as a commissioning advisor. Tim has a keen interest in evidence-based approaches to behavioral change, a topic that forms the foundation of much of his training work. Tim is writing his first novel.

CPSIA information can be obtained at www.ICGtesting.com
Printed in the USA
BVOW03s0846130215

387647BV00001B/64/P

9 780897 936965